R.

ACTION S[...]

Military Air[...]

Oxfordshire

ACTION STATIONS
Military Airfields of
Oxfordshire

Michael J.F.
Bowyer

Patrick Stephens

First published 1988

British Library Cataloguing in Publication Data

Bowyer, Michael J. F.
Action stations: Oxfordshire.
1. Air bases—England—Oxfordshire
—History   2. Oxfordshire—History,
Military
I. Title
358.4'17'094257   UG635.G7

ISBN 0-85059-824-9

Cover illustrations
Front *Photographic reconnaissance Spitfires, like this PR Mk XI,
were a common sight in Oxfordshire's wartime sky. Some
passed through Brize Norton's Aircraft Storage Unit and many
made deep sorties into Europe from Benson.* (RAF Museum/
Charles Brown Collection.) **Back** *Since 1970, F-111E swing-wing
bombers of the 20th Tactical Fighter Wing have operated
from Upper Heyford. USAF activity at the RAF station
commenced in 1950, on a lodger basis.* (US Air Force photo.)

*Patrick Stephens Limited is part of the
Thorsons Publishing Group, Denington Estate,
Wellingborough, Northamptonshire, NN8 2RQ, England*

Printed in Great Britain by Woolnough Bookbinding Limited,
Irthlingborough, Northamptonshire

1 3 5 7 9 10 8 6 4 2

CONTENTS

INTRODUCTION

A region situated between the Cotswolds and the Chiltern Hills and virtually bisected by the river Thames flanked by wet, low lying areas might be assumed to be unsuitable for airfields. Surprisingly that is quite untrue and by the end of the Second World War suitable sites had been found in Oxfordshire for 27 airfields.

Their origins differed. Some — like Bicester, Upper Heyford and Weston-on-the-Green — were updated products of the 1914-18 war. Upper Heyford and Bicester were rebuilt during the re-armament scheme of the mid-1920s in which the main British bomber force was placed in the South Midlands to be closer to France, the only feasible foe. Abingdon was an outcome of such thinking.

With more extensive re-armament in the mid-1930s came the building of another two bomber stations, Benson and Harwell. Oxfordshire's airfields would now contain much of Field Force France, the RAFs advanced bomber group. Due to their limited range its Fairey Battle bombers would attack Germany from bases in France, again an ally, and also support the British Expeditionary Force. Upper Heyford's Blenheims would serve the Air Component as a reconnaissance-bomber force working only with the BEF.

Before the war Oxfordshire was also moving into a support rather than an operational role. A very large aerodrome to accommodate a Flying Training School opened at Carterton, soon renamed Brize Norton to avoid confusion with existing Cardington. Although airfields were usually named after the parish in which their Station Headquarters were sited, it was sometimes necessary to re-title them to avoid confusion of one with another.

A second training station, a civilian one master-minded by Marshall of Cambridge, was built at Kidlington. Its purpose was to attract local young men prepared to volunteer for civilian or RAF reserve flying training thereby helping to form a very useful nucleus should war break out.

The considerable size of Brize Norton was partly the result of its additional use as a major Aircraft Storage Unit, No 6 Maintenance Unit. Particularly during the Battle of Britain and in the run-up to Operation Overlord, it played a most important part. Again, it had a civilian counterpart, for Lord Nuffield's interest in mass producing Spitfires not only resulted in the building of the huge Castle Bromwich factory at Birmingham. It also led to the establishment of No 1 Civilian Repair Unit and a small airfield by Morris Motors Cowley Works where Spitfires needing speedy repair and return to service were brought in large numbers, particularly in the summer of 1940. Similarly, de

Havilland had a 'CRU' at Witney for the repair of a variety of aircraft types, propellers and engines.

When the war started all the Oxfordshire-based squadrons moved to France. Their permanent aerodromes were vacant until, very soon, squadrons designated as training formations arrived. Into Bicester came Blenheims from Bassingbourn, for the training of crews for No 2 Group. Harwell became the home for two Wellington squadrons training personnel for No 3 Group. Benson received two squadrons of Whitleys, its task the preparation of aircrew for No 4 Group. Abingdon became an operational training centre for the Advanced Air Striking Force in France, and at Upper Heyford No 5 Group Pool handled the training of aircrew for Hampden squadrons. Benson's surface rapidly deteriorated and its heavy Whitleys were switched with Abingdon's Battles. With Kidlington and Weston-on-the Green serving as satellite airfields, and Brize Norton continuing as a pilot training school, the pattern for much wartime air activity over Oxfordshire was established.

Fear of air attacks destroying the pre-war, permanent stations, and a need to disperse aircraft, led in 1940 to the building of a number of satellite airfields. Among these were Finmere (for Bicester and Upper Heyford), Mount Farm (for Benson) and Stanton Harcourt (for Abingdon). All were used, particularly in the early years of the war, for night flying training. Although the volume of attack was less than expected there were some very sharp, damaging raids and intruder attacks on Oxfordshire's airfields.

An unusual change in air activity over the county came in 1941 following the decision to include the region in the Central Gliding Area. At nearby Haddenham the first Glider Training School was founded that year, then in July 1942 a huge operational conversion unit for glider pilots opened at Brize Norton. For many months unwieldy Whitleys towing awkward Horsa gliders were a sight which dominated the flying scene. This latest development established a new use for Oxfordshire's skies for since then RAF transport forces have either been based in the county or operated from close by. Need for a large number of glider pilots brought into use more airfields especially for initial glider flying training, and extended the county's commitment to training.

In 1942 Upper Heyford produced crews for Manchester bombers and soon began supplying them for Lancasters. The complexity of the four-engined aircraft and their increased crew compliments, which included flight engineers, led to re-planning of the bomber training scheme. As a result Wellingtons became the standard bomber types at Oxford's operational training units from which crews proceeded out of the region to heavy bomber conversion units. At Abingdon Whitley flying continued until late 1944, trained crews being needed for other roles as well as bombing.

From 1940 almost to the end of the war operational sorties for the purpose of dropping propaganda leaflets over France and providing diversion cover and feints were flown by the county's bomber OTUs. Most operational flying was, however, largely for a different purpose. In 1941 the ever expanding Photographic Reconnaissance Unit moved into Benson and Mount Farm. At the former on 13 July 1941 the RAF received its first Mosquito and on 17 September the first operational sortie by this, the most efficient warplane of all time, was flown from Benson. Thereafter PR Mosquitoes roamed to distant parts of Europe securing some of the most momentous of photographs including those of the V-weapons test centre at Peenemünde. From lonely flights by PR Spitfires came photographic proof that the Mohne Dam was breached, and much of the Ruhr was being shattered. To the close of hostilities Benson's role was of immense importance. Then its aircraft assisted in planning for rebuilding and mapped distant, strange places. From Benson emerged millions of photographic prints produced by continuous processing machines, forerunners of the type of equipment that produces our holiday pictures.

Before that, during the closing year of the war, Oxfordshire provided a base for airborne squadrons which took part in two great events. With its training role ended, Brize Norton, like Harwell and Broadwell, was one of the major stations from which the airborne invasion of Normandy was mounted. Come the autumn, partly from Oxfordshire, the Arnhem misadventure was despatched, following which a desperate need arose for replacement airborne forces. Again, glider training came under way at Brize Norton, after the operational squadrons moved eastwards to prepare for the Rhine crossing. Oxfordshire was once more a training and maintenance centre.

Immediate post-war years saw a gradual increase in the number of transport squadrons and associated units in the area. Abingdon's Yorks took part in the Berlin airlift, and operated long range trunk routes via Lyneham, before Oxfordshire entered a new aeronautical phase.

Agreement was reached in 1946 for the stationing of American bombers in Britain should the international situation ever require it. The USAF stated that, should such an event come about, it would prefer to operate from central England for that would allow defending fighters and missiles to provide a defensive shield in depth. Initially the B-29 Groups hastily brought to Britain in 1948 as a result of Russian intransigence and its imposition of the Berlin blockade, were based to the east. As soon as Upper Heyford and Brize Norton were enlarged and equipped to operate them and house their personnel, squadrons of B-29s, B-50s and later the jet B-47s made these airfields their temporary homes. Into Oxfordshire too droned gigantic B-36 eight-engined bombers, and later the first KC-135 tankers which replaced piston engined KB-29s and KC-97s, types which for some years were daily sights.

Come the intercontinental missile age and the US Strategic Air Command reduced its use of the Oxfordshire bases. Brize Norton once more became an RAF transport airfield and in the 1980s has become a base for giant in-flight refuelling tankers. Upper Heyford was switched to becoming a base for American tactical units and, after hosting a Wing of Voodoos, in September 1970 received the First F-111 swing-wing bombers for its 20th TFW. These operational aircraft have served in Oxfordshire for longer than any other type.

Over Oxfordshire flying has taken place almost from inception. There was interesting activity around its centre long before the 1914-18 war. The county has seen airships and cruise missiles in the form of V-1s pass overhead and watched some of the earlier British jet flying take place from Barford St John. It hosted the RAF's 50th Anniversary birthday party at Abingdon and houses the Queen's Flight. It played a major part in the Falklands conflict, and provided the base for a mighty portion of the western nuclear airborne deterrent in the 1950s and '60s. During the war the most important element of the British and US wartime photo reconnaissance force operated from Oxfordshire which is now the base for the essential RAF tanker force needed to maintain viable air defence of the United Kingdom. Scarcely a day passes without some distinctive sight of the American presence in the area. There is no question that Oxfordshire has had a very important aeronautical past and continues to play a major role in things aeronautical.

Acknowledgements

During the preparation of Action Stations 6 — upon which I have drawn for material for this volume — there were many who supplied items relating to Oxfordshire airfields. The RAF Museum, through R. W. Mack, was ever helpful; likewise the staff at Oxford County Library, at Oxford Mail and Radio Oxford. At the Atomic Energy Research Establishment, Harwell, I received much help especially from Peter Smallbone, Harry Coles, Norman Wallis, Denis Tyler and Eric Cannings who carried out extensive searches for material. To the USAF and its Magazine and Book Branch, the Imperial War Museum and Martin-Baker Ltd I am indebted for photographs.

Few books of this type can be written without the assistance of an army of fellow enthusiasts. Woven into this text are the gatherings of friends including Peter Corbell, Geoffrey Phillips MBE, John Rawlings and Ray Sturtivant, but a few of those who have over more than forty years exchanged with me their findings.

I am indeed grateful that I have been so fortunate to have enjoyed the fellowship of so many with interests similar to mine and to have often shared with them a ringside seat from which to view many an event recalled within these pages.

Michael J. F. Bowyer
Cambridge, September 1987

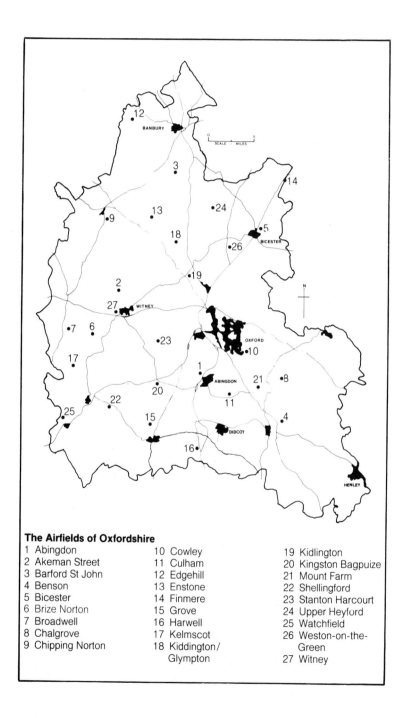

The Airfields of Oxfordshire

1 Abingdon
2 Akeman Street
3 Barford St John
4 Benson
5 Bicester
6 Brize Norton
7 Broadwell
8 Chalgrove
9 Chipping Norton

10 Cowley
11 Culham
12 Edgehill
13 Enstone
14 Finmere
15 Grove
16 Harwell
17 Kelmscot
18 Kiddington/
    Glympton

19 Kidlington
20 Kingston Bagpuize
21 Mount Farm
22 Shellingford
23 Stanton Harcourt
24 Upper Heyford
25 Watchfield
26 Weston-on-the-
    Green
27 Witney

THE AIRFIELDS

Abingdon

SU480990. 5 miles SW of Oxford, 1 mile NW of Abingdon town

Battle of Britain Day, 1967, the end of Abingdon's runway, weather appalling. Pity, for this was the last occasion when Abingdon's Beverley sisters would waggle their tails and much more in public. Abingdon was swathed in fog so dense that flying by the last of the largest aircraft the RAF ever operated in quantity was barely visible. It was no mean thrill to stand at the runway's edge as they emerged from the mist, wing tips soaring overhead before these dinosaur-like creatures floated into the fog, their wingtips showering water droplets. Five Beverleys soon crept in from the west and, in a style befitting a fighter, each one smoke-puffing, peeled off for a place in a stream landing. Memorable moments indeed.

RAF Abingdon has been an action station for over 50 years. Red brick, plentiful slate roofs and designs akin to army barracks of long ago, can be seen alongside assorted hangars and a large recent one built for the Beverleys. A 1925-style white-painted water tower competes with a stylish chimney of the 1930s.

Abingdon was once a simple airfield. In the plan approved on 20 July 1925 only 51 buildings were listed, four of them hangars of which three remain. Intended for two single-engined day bomber squadrons, facilities were provided for a Special Reserve Squadron in wartime. After slight alterations construction commenced in 1929, at the site whose surface shallow layer of loam rested upon a firm shale or clay base.

The station opened on 1 September 1932 under the Wessex Bombing Area. On 8 October 1932 the first aircraft arrived — Fairey Gordon single-engined biplane bombers of 40 Squadron. They had vacated Upper Heyford on 31 July

'Come on, let's be havin' yer'—from out of Building 108, one of Abingdon's 1920s style barrack blocks.

Left *Its excellent health belies its age, for Abingdon's water tower is of 1932 vintage.*

Below right *One of Abingdon's Hawker Harts, K3972, of XV Squadron, taking part in the 1935 Jubilee Review.*

Below *Fairey Gordons operated from both Abingdon and Upper Heyford in the early 1930s.*

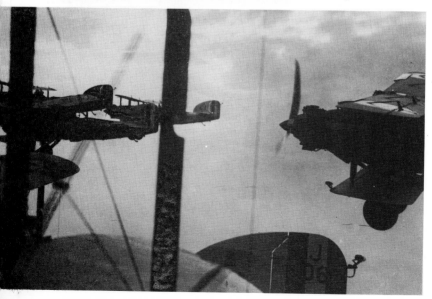

1932, flying here via armament training at Catfoss, the Squadron remaining until September 1939.

On 10 October 1932 the first permanent buildings were occupied, and Station Flight had an Atlas, Avro 504N and DH Moth by the end of the month. Oxford University Air Squadron moved in on 3 November for a long stay.

Central Area took control of Abingdon in November 1933. Only the Gordons were operating, but this was remedied on 1 June 1934 when XV Squadron formed and soon had Hawker Harts. In October 1935 40 Squadron re-equipped with Hart (Special) day bombers.

On 7 January 1936 there were clear signs of RAF expansion. More buildings were completed on the camp, and C Flight, 40 Squadron, became 104 Squadron. The following month, part of XV Squadron became the nucleus of 98 Squadron and received Hawker Hinds, more of which were delivered, to 40 Squadron, in March 1936.

Just over 2,000 people visited Abingdon's 1936 Empire Air Day viewing, among others, a Heyford, Overstrand, Bulldog, Moth and a stripped Tutor keeping company with two Hinds. For this treat they paid just one shilling, and saw some flying too. How many would now appear at Abingdon's gates for that show?

Abingdon was so crowded that in August 1936 both 98 and 104 Squadrons left from what had, since 1 May, been a 1 Group station. On 18 January 1937 XV Squadron parented No 52, a new Hind Squadron. On 3 May 1937, 62 Squadron arose from 40 Squadron. To make room for this latest formation 52 Squadron moved in late February to Upwood. On the 1937 Empire Air Day some 6,000 people called, and a new 12-Bay Type C Hangar was to be seen.

This was the period of considerable expansion of the RAF, in which Abingdon played a major part. Cranfield received 62 Squadron on 12 July 1937 when Avro Tutors of the Cambridge University Air Squadron were in summer camp at Abingdon. During November 1937 the Navy placed 802 Squadron on detachment here, its Hawker Nimrods and Ospreys staying until January 1938 when they boarded HMS *Glorious*. 40 Squadron shed a further Flight, on 3 March 1938 when 185 Squadron was reformed and

A Fairey Battle of XV Squadron flies over Abingdon shortly before the war. The airfield is central in the picture.

received Hinds, as did 106 Squadron, hived off from XV Squadron, on 1 June 1938.

On 13 June 1938, the first Fairey Battle arrived for XV Squadron which equipped with Battle IIs in June-July 1938. Seven Battles arrived for 40 Squadron on 7 July 1938, others for 106 Squadron following. The latter squadron and 18 Squadron left for Thornaby in August and September.

Both XV and 40 Squadrons, operational by late September 1938, formed a Wing of the Advanced Air Striking Force (AASF). Although 103 Squadron was here in September 1938 it was not earmarked, lack of equipment precluding 103 Squadron from joining.

With little warning both XV and 40 were placed at readiness on 10 September 1938 as the Munich Crisis developed. War preparations went ahead, short of mobilization. With conflict seeming inevitable, Station Commanders were, on 27 September, called to HQ 1 Group. Whilst they were meeting, the Prime Minister announced that war had been averted, bringing relief mixed with concern.

No 103 Squadron had received Battles between late July and mid-September 1938 and was fully operational before leaving in April 1939. Through spring and

summer 1939, Abingdon's squadrons trained for a role enacted when the Battle squadrons were ordered to prepare for France when Poland was invaded on 1 September 1939. By nightfall, civil aircraft had arrived to transport ground personnel. After being camouflaged, these aircraft set off at around 10:00 on 2 September. An hour later both squadrons followed to France as 71 Wing, AASF.

War station movement caused Whitley Is of 166 Squadron, and IIs of 97 Squadron to fly from Leconfield to Benson on 14 and 15 September 1939, while two Battle squadrons were to form an AASF Pool at Abingdon, 52 and 63 Squadrons arriving on 2 September 1939. Benson's surface was found unsuitable for Whitleys so a direct swop with Abingdon's Battles came about. Between 16 and 18 September, the Whitleys arrived forming 4 Group Pool. Former buildings of HQ 1 Group were taken over now, HQ 6 Group partly controlling bomber training replacing HQ 1 Group in vacated buildings. Both later became part of HQ 91 Group.

Whitley Mk IIIs replaced 166 Squadron's Mk Is in January 1940. On 23 March 1940 two visiting Whitleys landed back from the Ruhr, but the major event of the period occurred on 2 April when both

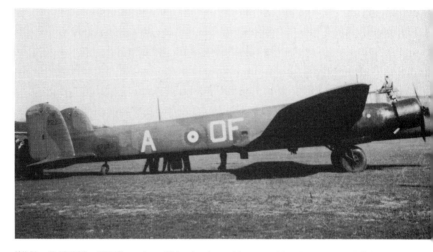

Whitley II, K7229, of 97 Squadron, Abingdon based between March and July 1940 by which time it was part of 10 OTU. On 5 March 1941, then with 10 B&GS, it crashed near Dumfries during a snowstorm.

Whitley squadrons dissolved into a new unit — No 10 Operational Training Unit. Whitleys of 97 and 166 Squadrons were placed in A Flight and Ansons of 97 Squadron with Whitleys of 166 Squadron formed B Flight. From May 1940 a few Merlin-engined Whitley IVs were at the station.

Débâcle in France caused some Battles to call at their one-time HQ airfield, and during the afternoon of 15 June no less than 73 AASF aircraft passed through, and six the next day.

By mid July 1940, 10 OTU's nominal establishment stood at forty, actual strength fourteen Whitleys and eighteen Ansons, the former in A, C and D Flights and the latter in B. 10 OTU first operated on 21 July 1940, dropping leaflets. More sorties were flown in August by Whitley IIIs and Vs. Tiger Whitleys, II and III, were then largely replaced by Mk Vs.

Abingdon's satellite, Stanton Harcourt, came into use for night flying on 3 September 1940 and remained under Abingdon's control until 15 January 1946. C Flight of 10 OTU began dispersing there on 10 September 1940 until a Whitley shortage brought disbandment in February 1941. A Flight, which converted

crews on to Whitleys, replaced it.

The importance of blind approach training brought about the formation of No 1 BAT Flight at Abingdon on 12 January 1941. It used Whitleys III and V and Ansons. Oxfords replaced Whitleys when 1501 BAT Flight was established in December 1941. The Flight moved to Stanton Harcourt on 18 April 1943, disbanding on 31 December 1943. Oxfords remained at Abingdon, within 91 Group Communications Flight.

Enemy intruders were active at dusk in the Oxford area on 12 March 1941. Whilst Whitleys were night flying, a raider dropped 16 bombs putting Abingdon out of action. Damage was caused to a Whitley, and other bombs fell around the bomb dump. The Germans came again, around 21:45 on 21 March 1941, dropping 26 bombs across 6 Group's HQ area. Seven offices were wrecked, ceilings and windows of another ten being damaged, in one of the few successful attacks on any HQ organization in Britain during the war.

Orders in May 1941 demanded that OTU output should be forty crews a month by using satellite facilities fully. 10 OTU now made use of Mount Farm, between 23 July 1941 and 12 February 1942. Availability of 10 OTU for leaflet drops was signalled in June 1941, and a few operational sorties were flown from Abingdon in July 1941.

OTU strength was around four dozen Whitleys and eighteen Ansons. In August 1941 Lysander target tugs were added, further aircraft of that type here at the end of the year being flown by 7 Anti-Aircraft Co-operation Unit.

Gradual replacement of front line Whitleys released them for alternative employment. Since late summer 1940 Whitley Vs had proven useful for ocean patrol, although the aircraft's attack profile was poor. To help to counter the U-Boats a special Whitley flight of 10 OTU formed in April 1942 and was placed at St Eval in Cornwall. Modifications to 33 aircraft enabled them to carry depth charges and also ASV radar. Operational flying was judged good for morale for, apart from eleven *Nickel* (ie leaflet dropping) sorties in November 1941 and eight in December, such flights were rare. Only four bombing sorties had been despatched — to Orleans and Tours airfields on 30 November 1941.

Simultaneous to using Whitleys for maritime purposes, 10 OTU was to participate in the 1,000 bomber raids. This depended upon crew availability as well as aircraft. Creaming off some for Biscay patrols was no help. Therefore, the detached flight delayed its operational debut, allowing 21 Whitleys to take off for Cologne on 30 May 1942. All returned, one crash landing at Manston. For the ensuing Essen raid, 22 Whitleys set out from Abingdon and one did not return. Abingdon's twenty-strong contingent for the June 1,000 Plan Bremen raid was less fortunate, three aircraft being lost and one crew was snatched from the sea.

St Eval's detachment began operational flying on 4 August 1942 with 26 aircraft. Each crew flew six operational patrols of nine to ten hours duration and for each was credited with a third of a bomber sortie. Four depth charges were carried and, to make each sortie really valuable, two 9½ lb practice bombs were aimed at a rock off the Cornish coast! A long range tank in the aircraft's belly extended its range. Crews were ordered to ditch if they met one of the Ju 88s now patrolling Biscay making it little wonder that a popular song became questionably 'I'm dreaming of a White Whitley ...' Operations ceased on 19 July 1943. When the detachment returned to Abingdon on 23 July 1943 it had flown 1,862 sea patrols, 16,864 flying hours, had 91 U-Boat sightings, made 55 attacks, damaged *U-214, U-523* and *U-591* and sunk the *U-564*. Aircraft losses totalled 33.

Participation in Main Force raids on Germany, code named *Grand National*, took place in summer 1942. Targets were in Bremen, Düsseldorf and Essen. Operational training was then resumed, interspersed with a few leaflet dropping sorties in February and April 1943.

Strength of 10 OTU in February 1943 was 55 Whitley V, eleven Ansons, three Lysanders and one Defiant. Earlier needs to night fly at the satellite to avoid bombing of the parent station being no longer necessary, the unit was re-organized, A and B Flights being at Stanton Harcourt and C, D and G at Abingdon. In April 1943, Martinets replaced the Lysanders. *Bullseyes* (massed night bombing and anti-aircraft co-operation exercises) were being flown and ASR sorties. 91 Group Air Gunners Instructors' School opened, giving a seven-day course and employing two Whitleys and two Martinets. Some of the 54 Whitleys at 10 OTU in August 1943 were Mk VIIs retrieved from St Eval. *Nickelling* was carried out in September 1943, a dozen such sorties being flown in November and sixteen in December without loss.

Into 1944 Whitleys droned around Abingdon, managing twelve sorties to France in January 1944 to drop 2,266,000 leaflets. During one operation Sergeant Averill was 25 miles into France when an engine failed. All removable equipment was jettisoned before the Whitley landed safely at Tangmere. In February 1944, 10 OTU flew 13 more sorties, dropping 1,656,144 leaflets, the most by one unit that month. A disturbing feature, though, was the loss of Whitley

LA787 sent to St Quentin on 28 February 1944. Whitleys subsequently operated west of the north/south line passing through Paris, and only OTU Wellingtons ventured eastwards. In March 1944 another dozen *Nickel* sorties were flown.

Until 20 March 1944, Abingdon's Whitleys operated from grass runways. Flying was then switched to Stanton Harcourt whilst two runways were laid at the parent station. It was at its satellite that 10 OTU bade farewell to its faithful old Whitleys, and unit establishment reduced to three-quarters OTU. Four Hurricanes replaced the Martinets during June and, in July 1944, 10 OTU commenced re-equipping with Wellington Xs. Not until October 1944 did the last Whitley leave 10 OTU. Daylight flying was resumed at Abingdon on 16 November 1944.

In March 1945 10 OTU's strength stood at fifty Wellington Xs, five Hurricanes and two Master IIs. Remaining in 91 Group, 10 OTU did not disband until 10 September 1946.

Abingdon's bomber link was broken on 24 October 1946 when Transport Command look control and 525 Squadron moved in. On 1 December it was renumbered 238 Squadron. No 46, here by the start of 1947, also flew Dakotas. All vacated Abingdon in December 1947 and were replaced by Avro Yorks of Nos 51, 59 and 242 Squadrons, operating overseas trunk routes. In December 1947, eight months after disbandment at Shallufa, 40 Squadron reformed at Abingdon, its ancestral home.

When the Russians blockaded Berlin, Yorks played a major part in the air lift. On 10 July 1948, the first York to arrive in Berlin was one of Abingdon's 59 Squadron. The Yorks were soon sited at German airfields, reducing expense and increasing the supply rate. When the Berlin airlift ended, Abingdon was switched to an army support role, the station moving from 47 to 38 Group on 27 June 1949. The York squadrons left for Bassingbourn, apart from 242 Squadron which re-equipped with Hastings. Both the TCDU and ATrDU moved to Abingdon and, in 1950, No 1 Parachute Training School came from Upper Heyford, complete with its famous parachutists' tower and captive balloon. This move was brought about to allow the rebuilding of Upper Heyford for the USAF.

No 30 Squadron's Valettas arrived in November 1950 and stayed until May 1952. A 1951 arrival was No 1 Overseas Ferry Unit complete with Harvards, Oxfords and Mosquitoes for training. It was responsible for delivery of aircraft overseas and became best known for the trans-Atlantic delivery of Sabre jets to the RAF. On 1 February 1953 the OFU split into two squadrons, Nos 147 and 167, before moving to Benson in April 1953. Transport Command Air Support Flight, known from 14 September 1954 as 1312 Flight, replaced them.

Familiar sight of the 1960s, Beverley XB287 passing and bearing the Abingdon arms on its nose.

Above *Beverleys of 47 Squadron resting at Abingdon in 1964. Fairing doors were removed to permit heavy load drops.*

Below *Its the biggest, final fly past in the world, as 'our Gracie' might have sung. Beverleys singing their last farewell on 16 September 1967 at Abingdon's Battle of Britain Display.*

Abingdon was 46 Squadron's home when it was equipped with Andover C.1s.

In May 1953 Abingdon assumed an operational role with the arrival of Hastings of Nos 24 and 47 Squadrons from Topcliffe and Dishforth. No 53 Squadron replaced No 24 on 1 January 1957, then ferried troops to Kenya for anti-Mau Mau operations.

March 1956 saw the arrival of 162 ft span Beverleys, able to carry bulky loads and operate from small, rough airstrips. In February 1957, 53 Squadron received its first Beverleys and, on 28 June 1963, merged with 47 Squadron, crews drawing their aircraft from a central pool. Abingdon, with over 2,000 aircraft movements a month, had become one of the busiest airfields in Britain. The long F Hangar was handed over to the RAF on 30 April 1959, and ten years later was modified to permit Belfasts to come for overhauls.

Until 31 October 1967, Beverleys of 47/53 Squadron operated world wide while the Transport Command Air Movements Development Unit carried out research into movements of heavy freight and large scale air movements.

In the summer of 1966 the station became the base for the Andover Training Flight. On 1 December 1966 the first Andover Squadron formed, No 46, and was stationed here until it moved to Thorney Island in August 1970 along with the Training Flight. No 52 Squadron, Andover equipped, also formed here on 1 December 1966 and soon went overseas.

April 1968 was mutely celebrated as the RAF's 50th birthday, amid ill feeling towards a government reckoned to be unsympathetic to the RAF and certainly oblivious of tradition. Whilst one intrepid soul flew by the Houses of Parliament at a low level in an attempt to wake the incumbents, others conserved their energy for HM Queen Elizabeth's visit to the RAF on 14 June 1968. The venue for the event, marked by a large exhibition of historic aircraft, many destined for the Hendon museum, was Abingdon where HM Queen Elizabeth II lunched appropriately in an Officers' Mess dating back to Imperial days.

On 1 September 1972 the Air Support

Andover C.1 XS609 is depicted in its curious kneeling position permitting easy rear access. July, 1969.

Command Examining Unit became 46 Group Air Transport Examining Unit, Strike Command. The Joint Air Transport Establishment, formed here in 1971, moved from Abingdon to Brize Norton on 31 December 1975 followed by PTS, for on 1 January 1976 the station was transferred from 38 Group to RAF Support Command. The 600 ft long, 140 ft wide, 50 ft high unique 'F' hangar became the centre for Jaguar overhaul and repair by the Aircraft Production Squadron. Lecon-field's 60 MU and 71 MU Bicester, had amalgamated to form the Engineering Wing in May 1976, and the first of many Jaguars to pass through arrived on 3 June 1976. Hawks are now handled.

In addition to Nos 1 and 2 Aircraft Maintenance Squadron, the Repair and Salvage Squadron is based here to maintain fixed wing aircraft in Britain and overseas. Since August 1973 Bulldogs of the University of London Air Squadron have resided alongside Chipmunks of No

Stored at Abingdon VC 10s were in 1983 wrapped in gigantic black bags.

6 Air Experience Flight. In 1975 they were joined by Oxford UAS whose Bulldogs were brought from Bicester. Abingdon has hosted VC10s withdrawn from British Airways and stored for military use.

Akeman Street

SP335140. 3 miles NW of Witney
Akeman Street's title dates from 2,000 years ago when a Roman road passed across England, its line running over this wartime airfield. Akeman Street's site was selected in late 1939 for development into a Relief Landing Ground (RLG) for 2 Service Flying Training School Brize Norton, and was available from 10 July 1940. Following the bombing of Brize Norton, the Advanced Training Squadron of 2 SFTS came here and, two days after

*Akeman Street, a grass surfaced Relief Landing Ground affiliated to Little Rissington, straddled the Roman Road from which it took its name. Three landing strips were available, N–S (1,100 yd), NE–SW (950 yd) and SE–NW (800 yd). **A** Bellman hangar (Type 5490/36) **B** Ten 65 ft Over Type Blister hangars (Type 12512/41) **C** Dining room and mess facilities **D** Black camouflaging lines applied to the grass to represent hedgerows.*

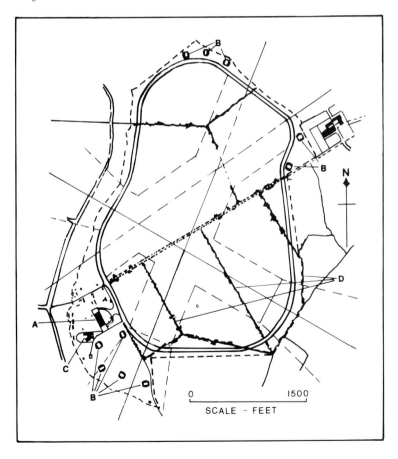

0   1500
SCALE – FEET

23

the raid, was a going concern.

By March 1941, Oxfords of 2 SFTS were also making considerable use of Southrop. An Oxford, night flying near Akeman Street at 03:30 hours on 28 July 1941, was brought down some two miles north-east of the airfield by an intruder. Such incidents were, fortunately, rare.

Flying by 2 SFTS Oxfords continued until March 1942. On 14 March, 2 SFTS was re-designated 2 (Pilots) Advanced Flying Unit.

The training syllabus changed, for the main task of a (Pilots) Advanced Flying Unit was to accustom those trained overseas to the complications of flying over Europe occasioned by the intensity of activity and inclement weather. The Airspeed Oxfords remained until 14 July 1942 when 2 (P) AFU closed. By then the flying field had more of the appearance of a modestly developed airfield. Living quarters, mess buildings, shelters and a small operations block had been built by Laing, with help from Thorn. Most buildings were to 1941 designs, including ten Over Type 65 ft Blister hangars (pattern 12512/41) and a large Bellman of older style than most, (5498/36). Although small, three grass runways were closely sited on the field overlapping for much of their area.

After 2 (P) AFU closed, the airfield was allocated to 6 (P) AFU, Little Rissington, which started using the site in July 1942 and continued to do so until October 1945 although flying ceased on 15 August 1945. Still in the hands of Flying Training Command, it closed on 1 February 1947. Crop sprayers sometimes operate from the site.

Barford St John

SP440340. SE of Bloxham, NW of Deddington, off the B4031 at Hempton
A well-guarded central area containing tall radio masts marks Barford as a 'communications centre'. A board near the camp entrance informs the passerby that it is the home of a 'Transmitter Annexe' in Anglo-American hands. More thrilling moments in its life are left to imagination.

Barford came into use in mid-1941 as a small, grass Relief Landing Ground which, on 30 June 1941, Oxfords of 15 SFTS Kidlington began using for practice flying. Late on 24 August an enemy aircraft dropped six light bombs on the east side of the landing ground, but it caused little disturbance.

By late 1941 a decision had been taken to develop the airfield extensively. A conventional three-runway pattern was imposed, with 'T2' hangars, and temporary wartime brick buildings. Bomber Command took control on 10 April 1942 and made Barford into Upper Heyford's satellite, re-opening it on 15 December 1942 with Wellington IIIs of 16 OTU. March 1943 brought Mustang 1s of Nos 4 and 169 Squadrons for their part in exercise *Spartan*. Fast as they were, the Mustangs would have found themselves outshone had they stayed for a few weeks.

Early plans for flying jet aircraft highlighted basic problems. Gloster's airfield at Brockworth was too small for experimental aircraft whose power plants seemed likely to enforce long, problematic take off runs. The company shopped around for suitable test centres, first using Cranwell and then Newmarket Heath. Another airfield extensively used was Barford St John.

Gloster's were afforded the use of half a hangar at Barford in May 1943, and the station became the flight test centre for the Gloster F.9/40, basis of the Meteor. To Barford came, also, the Gloster E.28/39 'Pioneer' *W4041*, the first British jet aircraft, by then fitted with the more powerful W.2/500 engine. Between 12 and 29 June 1943 it managed 23 flights from Barford, and also received high-speed aerofoil section wings. *W4041* left late 1943 for Farnborough to continue engine and aerodynamic testing.

On Sunday, 28 May 1943, the Halford-engined F.9/40, *DG206* flew in from Newmarket Heath. *DG205* fitted with W.2B engines first flew from here, on 12 June 1943 and throughout the summer both aircraft were active. F.9/40, *DG204*, with underslung axial flow Metrovick F/2 engines, arrived in August 1943. It

By Gloster F.9/40 DG205/G stand famous folk connected with the early days of jet flying. Left to right: Gloster test pilots Crosby Warren and Michael Daunt; Mr F. MacKenna, Gloster's Managing Director; Air Commodore Sir Frank Whittle and Mr W. G. Carter (model jet pipe in hand?), Gloster's Chief Designer.

never flew from Barford, trouble being encountered with high idling thrust which would have made control at slow speed very difficult. F.9/40s flew from Barford until Gloster's acquired Moreton Valence.

Jet flying only took place in good, calm weather. It had to be slotted into the busy training programme carried out at Barford by 16 OTU's Wellington IIIs, and later its Mk Xs. The gunnery element of 16 OTU was also placed here.

Good reserves of aircrew halted 16 OTU's Wellington flying on 12 December 1944 and brought a dramatic change, for Mosquitoes of 1655 Mosquito Training Unit — mainly Mks XX, XXV and TIII — arrived on 30 and 31 December 1944 at the parent station, and at Barford where most of the TIIIs were based, accompanied by Oxfords. From 1 January 1945 the unit was known as 16 OTU and prepared Mosquito crews for 8 Group. This continued until the summer of 1945 when

flying was reduced. Mosquito XVIs replaced the Canadian-built Mosquitoes in mid-summer 1945.

Positioning of lights to control traffic passing the end of the main runway at Barford received much publicity in July 1945, but within a few weeks Barford was lying rejected. The move of 16 OTU to Cottesmore in March 1946 caused it to cease being an active airfield.

Benson

SU631910. 13 miles SE of Oxford close to the A423(T)

Benson will be remembered as the home of photographic reconnaissance and the most magical aeroplane of all — the de Havilland Mosquito. Both flourished here from 1941 to 1953. From Benson the Mosquito made its operational debut, and soon its Mosquitoes regularly roamed across Europe. They left from here to secure those famous photographs of

The names Mosquito and Benson are almost synonymous, for from Benson the Mosquito made its operational debut. The prototype PR Mk 1 W4051 served at the station. (DH.)

Peenemünde, V-1s and 2s, and even reached the Balkans on unarmed sorties requiring colossal courage. Single-handed pilots of Benson's Spitfires often called on Berlin and took the shots that proved the Möhne Dam had been breached. Most important of all, it was Benson's crews who had the responsibility for finding just how effective the colossal wartime investment in Bomber Command was proving to be.

Building of Benson commenced in 1937 on a fine site through which a public road passes unusually above the level of four 'C' Type hangars. Occupation of the station came early in 1939 and, during the first days of April, Nos 103 and 150 Squadrons brought their Battles for a

five-month stay. On 2 September 1939, they left for France, as part of the AASF.

The intention was that, upon the outbreak of hostilities, Whitleys of 97 and 166 Squadrons would form 4 Group Pool here. But Benson's grass surface was found unsuitable when a detachment from 166 Squadron tried it. Therefore, on 9 September 1939, plans changed. Nos 52 and 63 Battle Squadrons and a few Ansons moved to Benson and the Whitleys went to Abingdon.

On arrival they found themselves alongside Airspeed Envoy *G-AEXX* of the King's Flight, for Hendon was no longer suitable for the Flight whose commander had wanted a move to Smith's Lawn in Windsor Great Park. Lacking range and defensive armament, the Envoy was the subject of concern, so, in the summer of 1939, a Lockheed Hudson, N7263, was chosen for the King's use. Internal modifications were made and its bulbous dorsal turret was retained. Extra tanks extended the range to 3,000 miles, although only one passenger could be conveyed. Normal bomber camouflage was retained and there was no identity other than roundels and a serial number. King's Flight officers preferred using two Albatross airliners G-AEVV and G-AEVW but the suggestion was turned down. At Benson the Flight relied on the Hudson. March 1940 saw the arrival of a Percival Q.6 from Northolt for the King who shared it with the AOC Bomber Command. A second Hudson, N7364, held for a month early in 1940, was an unmodified reserve.

Meanwhile, both Battle squadrons had become part of 1 Group Pool, abnormally increased by the arrival of 207 Squadron from Cranfield in April 1940. The three squadrons then amalgamated to form No 12 Operational Training Unit whose Armament Training Flight was permanently detached to Penrhos for live weapons practice.

Benson's defences were rapidly strengthened in June 1940, pillboxes being constructed around the perimeter. At 23:55 on 29 June 1940, eighteen High Explosive bombs (HEs) fell in the vicinity of the fully lit station during a high level attack. It caused the satellite station, Mount Farm, to be put to use before intended.

July found the OTU training Battle crews to replace those lost in France. On 13 August the first Polish airmen arrived, to be trained for new Battle squadrons. As the Poles were welcomed as befits the brave people they have always been, the enemy also paid his compliments. A Ju 88 dived out of low cloud, dropping three HEs and an oil bomb. One HE fell upon unoccupied Shelter No 12 hurling debris on to the roof of the Airmen's Mess and between 'C' and 'D' hangars where an Anson was damaged. Two other bombs fell on waste ground and the oil bomb failed to ignite. Construction of a perimeter track commenced in August,

and September's duty concentrated upon training Poles and Czechs.

Brief trials with a Stirling showed the unsuitability of the grass airfield surface for such heavy aircraft, and there was doubt as to whether it would permit even Wellingtons which, by mid-November, were intended for 12 OTU. Cranfield and Twinwood were alternative sites for 12 OTU but, by November, Mount Farm had metalled runways making this satellite quite suitable for Wellington day and night flying, leaving Benson available for maintenance duties and day flying. Benson was re-organised with effect from 1 December 1940, the OTU strength changing to the equivalent of a half heavy bomber OTU. The Poles and Battles were posted away.

Establishment of 12 OTU was reduced to give space to No 1 Photographic Reconnaissance Unit from Heston. Completed on 27 December 1940, its arrival brought strange, unusually coloured Spitfires to Benson for work still of an experimental nature. Blenheim IV's and a few Hudsons accompanied them. Wellingtons were meanwhile arriving for 12 OTU which commenced training with them on 4 January 1941, taking in six complete crews per fortnight.

A special award was made at this time to two soldiers, Sergeant D. Jobson and Private E. D. Gurnham, RASC. Each was given a George Medal for courage in getting a pilot from a burning Battle on 14 July 1940.

Airfield extension was decided upon before 30 January, when in the early afternoon, nineteen HE bombs and incendiaries fell within the airfield boundary without causing damage. On 27 February 1941 an enemy aircraft strafed and bombed the aerodrome and destroyed a Wellington.

By March 1941 the average intake at 12 OTU had fallen to only four crews a fortnight. Hopes for a regular six had been curtailed because the OTU was converting 1 Group Battle squadron crews to Wellingtons. Bad winter weather and the thaw played havoc with the landing ground surface, bringing the loss of three Wellingtons in a month, one over-running its chocks and smashing into No 1 Hangar.

As winter passed, Spitfire PR operations increased. On 10 April 1941, for instance, a Spitfire was shot down on a sortie to Brest whilst another managed to secure PRUs first photographs of Copenhagen. Meanwhile, Flight Lieutenant A. L. Taylor was photographing Le Bourget, after which he strafed the airfield. Four days later, Sergeant W. Morgan managed an incredible feat when, in a Spitfire, he photographed Genoa and Spetzia before landing at Hawkinge in Kent after a seven hour ten minute flight at the end of which he had only two gallons of petrol left. He had established a record for such operations.

On the previous day, Pilot Officer S. H. Dowse had been less fortunate when four Bf 109s intercepted his Spitfire over Bergen. After escaping, he courageously turned into Germany, came out over Wilhelmshaven and forced landed, short of fuel, near Ipswich after an action-packed five-hour flight. April's successful sorties totalled 55, and a further 79 were flown in May. Wellingtons of 12 OTU in June 1941 flew a few *Nickels*. On 17 June, No 1 PRU established another record for, in the course of thirteen successful sorties, 37 films were run from which 6,800 prints were made between 12:30 hours and 22:10 hours. Marylands were, at this time, coming to Benson to be fitted with cameras, prior to operating in the Mediterranean Theatre.

No 12 OTU began to move to Chipping Warden on 10 July 1941 depriving itself of witnessing that exhilerating moment when, on 13 July, No 1 PRU received its first Mosquito. Benson's PR strength was further expanded when five Spitfires and a Blenheim IV of No 3 PRU arrived from Oakington to become part of 1 PRU which surrendered Mount Farm to 15 OTU. By early September 1941 12 OTU had completely moved into Chipping Warden, and Benson had come under Coastal Command control.

It was to Squadron Leader R. F. H. Clerke that the honour fell on 17 September of being the first pilot to take a Mosquito *(W4055)* on an operational sortie during which he called upon Bordeaux, La Pallice and Brest. Flight Lieutenant Taylor took the aircraft on its second operation, three days later, to the Heligoland-Sylt area. Already, the Mosquito was ranging widely.

Fast times and long duration were common to Benson's complement whose aircraft nearly always flew without defensive armament. Two long Mosquito flights, of 12 and 28 February 1942, were to Danzig and Gdynia in Poland, respectively. By March, Mosquitoes were largely handling the Scandinavian commitment, leaving Spitfires to other areas. There were, though, notable exceptions such as a brave low-level run by Victor Ricketts and Boris Lukhmanoff to photograph the bombed Renault works at Billancourt. Augsburg, too, was photographed in April 1942 following the Lancaster low-level daylight raid on the MAN works. Damage assessment flights to Germany were mainly flown by individualistic Spitfire IVs.

In September 1940 a de luxe DH Flamingo, *R2766*, had arrived for the King's Flight. Alongside its RAF roundels it carried the civil registration *G-AGCC* to enable it to cross neutral territory in an emergency. Group Captain Fielden pressed for a communications aircraft and, curiously, was offered the captured Me 108 *G-AFRN*, held at Farnborough. Displeasure greeted this and instead a Tutor, *K6120*, which had joined 63 Squadron at Benson in November 1939 and passed to 12 OTU, was put at the Flight's disposal. The Flamingo raised a number of problems, for it was an unarmed unfamiliar shape needing a fighter escort so it was disposed of to 24 Squadron. Questions then arose about the continued existence of the King's Flight, and it was decided that it would disband. The King would fly in aircraft provided by a VIP detachment of 24 Squadron based at Northolt. Disbandment took place at Benson on 14 February 1942. The Hudson, *N7263*, which had been used as the Royal aircraft early in the war joined 161 Squadron at Tempsford, and the Percival Q6 left for Halton in May 1942.

Mosquitoes often returned to Benson with photographs of amazing quality and of very distant places. Depicted here is the Augsburg Messerschmitt factory, photographed on 24 April 1942.

Another squadron which used Benson in the winter of 1941–42 was No 140. Formed to provide photographic coverage of enemy movements during an invasion of Britain, and as 1416 Flight based at Hendon, it gradually became a strategic reconnaissance unit for GHQ Home Command, controlled by Army Co-operation and not Coastal Command. It moved to Benson early in September 1941 with a mixture of Spitfires, with Blenheim IVs for night duty. Operations over coastal France commenced on 1 October 1941 and, in November, night operations by the Blenheims

started, during which they took photographs by the light of flash bombs. Another task was photographic support of the army within Britain, particularly of its use of camouflage. Early in 1942 the squadron began to photograph Channel shipping, until 4 May when the squadron's entire establishment and role changed. Next day it moved to Mount Farm to concentrate on army strategic reconnaissance over France, making flights leading to the Dieppe landing. The move had another purpose for, as 140 Squadron left Benson, the building of concrete runways began.

Clear, summer weather allowed a great increase in successful photographic reconnaissance operations. No 1 PRU expanded fast, frequently detaching aircraft to other bases at home and abroad. For administrative purposes the PR force was re-organized into squadrons rather than a series of Flights. The Unit dispersed on 18 October 1942, its dozen Mosquitoes equipping 540 Squadron while fourteen Spitfire PR IVs became 541 Squadron, an assortment of nineteen Spitfires became 542 Squadron and another 15 changed into 543 Squadron, leaving a mixture of Marylands, Ansons, Spitfires and Wellington IVs to call themselves 544 Squadron.

Benson was certainly an action station, despatching sorties over the whole of Europe. At nearby Medmenham, results were analysed. The Battle of the Ruhr was daily recorded and, at 07:25 hours on 17 May 1943, Flying Officer F. G. Fray set off in Spitfire IV, *EN343*, of 542 Squadron to photograph the results of the attacks on the Mohne and Sorpe Dams. Next day Flying Officer D. G. Scott took *EN411* over the Ruhr to observe and photograph the extent of flooding of the Ruhr and on the following day Benson Spitfires flew another three sorties to the Sorpe Dam. During their ever-deeper penetrations into Germany, Mosquitoes of 540 Squadron returned with photographs of Peenemünde which confirmed its use and, for the British, the development of the V-weapons. Experimental night photography using Mosquito IVs of 544

Squadron began in February 1943.

Two-stage supercharged Merlin engines led to refinements of both Spitfires and Mosquitoes. The Spitfire PR Mk XI came into use at Benson in May 1943 and a handful of re-engined Mosquito Mk IVs, redesignated PR VIIIs, had been introduced in February 1943. In June, 540 Squadron began operating PR IXs.

During October 1943, 543 Squadron left Benson. Spitfires of 541 and 542 Squadron and Mosquitoes of 544 Squadron and 540 Squadron stayed until March 1945. Before 543 Squadron vacated Benson its 'B' Flight was hived off to form the nucleus of 309 Ferry Training Unit, also known as 309 Ferry Training and Aircraft Despatch Unit, and which held a few Master IIs and Spitfire IVs for the training of pilots prior to their ferrying reconnaissance Spitfires overseas.

Frequent attempts were made to photograph the German capital, at the start of 1944 and throughout the Battle of Britain. Then Benson began to play a vital role in the run-up to the invasion of France with 544 Squadron photographing much of northern France. Both Benson's Mosquito squadrons employed pressure cabin Mark XVIs from the middle of 1944. The Spitfire squadrons used a few Mustang IIIs and received the first of their Griffon-engined PR Mk XIX Spitfires. In midsummer 1944 the strength of Benson's four operational squadrons was 80 aircraft. A few were detached to Dyce in August, and also to the USSR, to observe the movements of the battleship *Tirpitz*

After the war Mosquito PR 34s carried out survey and reconnaissance work from Benson, much for civilian purposes. PF669:OT-L of 58 Squadron was an aircraft used for this work.

Mosquitoes and Spitfire PR 19s were used post war by Benson's Photographic Reconnaissance Development Unit.

for Bomber Command.

At the end of hostilities Benson had a few very long range Mosquito PR 34s, and had despatched this aircraft's first operational sortie (by 544 Squadron) to Norway on 7 May 1945. Unlike most operational stations, however, Benson had an exceptionally busy period ahead. Damage assessment flights over Europe were needed in plenty so that rehabilitation and rebuilding could commence after the tremendous destruction wrought in the closing months of the war. Photographic sorties were also flown over Britain, Malta and a variety of overseas territories. Benson became the centre to which such agencies as the Ministry of Agriculture, and of Town and County Planning, could turn for help. Techniques of war were being put to vital peacetime service.

Such was the quantity of material required that Benson's mechanical processing equipment, such as the continuous processing units coupled to fast drying techniques, were as useful as in the closing stages of the war. Advances in survey photography had been amazing. Processing had changed from little more than hand development to machines churning out thousands of prints in a day. The value of photography for mapping purposes, particularly of uncharted areas, became an adjunct to the activities at Benson as a result of which a handful of Lancasters were acquired and, on 1 October 1946, became part of a new 82 Squadron at Benson. They spent much time overseas photographing vast tracts of Africa.

No 542 Squadron disbanded on 27 August 1945, and 544 Squadron on 13 October 1945. On 30 September 1946, 540 and 541 Squadrons were both disbanded. From them arose No 58 Squadron, manned and equipped by the old hands and armed with Mosquito PR 34s and Ansons modified for survey work. A new 541 Squadron was formed in November 1947 and another 540 Squadron the following month. The former operated Spitfire PR XIXs in a tactical role, the latter equipped with Mosquito PR 34s for strategic reconnaissance. For

31

night photographic duty, 58 Squadron received specialized Mosquito PR 35s.

It was not only the needs of civilians which had to be answered after the war. Belligerence in the East caused all sorts of devices to be used, under the label of 'reconnaissance'. Specialized training was essential for reconnaissance crews, for which purpose 8 OTU was retained and variously flew from Mount Farm, Chalgrove and Benson. It became 237 OCU on 31 July 1947 and did not leave the area until the start of December 1951, by then equipped not with Harvards and Spitfire XIXs but with Meteor 7s and 9s and Mosquito PR 34s.

Jet aircraft were late on the reconnaissance scene in Britain, the intended Meteor V proving troublesome. Later Meteors were little more than short duration tactical aircraft and not until the first Canberra PR 3s reached 540 Squadron at Benson, at the end of 1952, was the PR force moving into the new age. Meteor PR 10s had joined 541 Squadron just before it left for Germany in mid-June 1951.

At the end of October 1952, 82 Squadron's Lancasters returned to Benson, among them the famous Lancaster *PA474* which thrills us as part of the Battle of Britain Memorial Flight. The squadron's stay was brief for, in March 1953 along with the other PR units and squadrons at Benson, it moved to Wyton. A great era at Benson had ended, and the station would never again host anything like it.

Transfer to RAF Transport Command took place in March 1953 and Benson became an aircraft despatch centre. 30 Squadron operating Valettas was briefly here before moving to Dishforth. Two squadrons with similar roles, Nos 147 and 167, arrived at Benson in April 1953 and later amalgamated to become the Ferry Squadron. An unexpected event was the reforming of No 21 Squadron here on 1 May 1959, its duty reminiscent of the RAFs pre-war policing activity overseas. It trained at Benson with four Twin Pioneers before leaving in mid-September 1959.

There had been an even more unlikely occupant in the mid-1950s when the Southern Air Division arrived from Culham in July 1953, Culham being unsuitable for jet fighters, No 1832 Squadron, RNVR, which set up shop here in July 1955 to fly Attackers, shared them with 1836 Squadron. In October 1956 Sea Hawk 1s started to replace the Attackers, but the Navy's stay was brief, for on 10 March 1957 the squadrons were paid off.

Transport Command had important plans for Benson. The new medium-range, unconventional-looking, tail-loaded Argosy twin-boom freighter was being prepared, intended to be able to reach Cyprus non-stop fully loaded. Benson was chosen as the UK base for Argosy squadrons. Here the first Argosy

Briefly Benson based were Valettas of No 30 Squadron.

As Culham was unsuitable for jets the Southern Air Division, the Royal Navy's reserve formation embracing 1832 and 1846 Squadrons, operated its Attackers from Benson in 1956. Mk 2 WP289 '862' is illustrated.

for RAF service arrived on 18 November 1961, for a training unit which became 242 Operational Conversion Unit before leaving for Thorney Island in April 1963.

No 114 Squadron reformed at Benson on 1 October 1961 to operate the Argosy equipment, commencing in February 1962 at the same time as 105 Squadron received Argosies. It flew them for four months before moving overseas. No 267 Squadron began to equip in November 1962 and continued to operate from Benson until the Argosy's withdrawal and the squadron disbanded on 30 June 1970. Another recipient had been 215 Squadron which worked up on Argosies at Benson between May and August 1963. With the disbandment of 114 Squadron on 31 October 1971, Benson's troop and freight transport role was ended — but not that of passenger carrying.

Royal wartime flying was the task of 24 Squadron and later of the Metropolitan

Sea Hawk F.1s, including WF173, replaced the Attackers of Southern Air Division in the autumn of 1956.

A fair proportion of the RAF's Argosy fleet tied up at Benson in 1969 when its voyage through life was ended.

Communications Squadron. The King thought highly of their Dakotas and, in a world where flying was ever increasing, the King's Flight was reformed at Benson on 1 May 1946. Air Commodore Fielden resumed his Captaincy. Originally the King's Flight was to operate a VVIP (Very Very Important Person) York and three Vikings, two with VVIP fit and the other with the normal passenger layout. Instead, only four cheaper Vikings were allotted, the additional one serving as an engineering support aircraft. To speed delivery, BEA surrendered two early Vikings allowing one as *VL245* — the normal passenger aircraft — to be collected from Wisley for the Flight on 11 August 1946. It joined Dominie *RL951*, already in use and whose career abruptly ended in a crash at Mount Farm in November 1946. All four Vikings were at Benson by January 1947 and a month later flew to Brooklyn Air Base, near Capetown from where they operated during the South

The Argosy remained in service long enough for a few to receive two-tone brown/black camouflage. A few carried bombs on stub wings and operated during the Aden troubles.

African Royal Tour. Later in 1947 they were busy during the wedding of Princess Elizabeth and Prince Philip, and subsequently many times carried the Royal Family.

Prince Philip commenced flying lessons in 1952. Using Chipmunk WP861, he made his first solo flight on 20 December 1952. Subsequently he flew another Benson-based Chipmunk, WP912, and then made use of Devon VP961, stationed at White Waltham from which airfield he had undertaken most of his flying training. For Queen's Flight purposes the Devon was too small, yet it was a reliable and pleasant aircraft for pilot and passengers for which reason one of its larger derivatives, a Heron, was ordered for Prince Philip.

Vikings remained very active but the little-used workshop aircraft was disposed of in November 1953 when the future of the Flight was under review. A plan emerged by which the Heron would reach the Flight early in 1954, and the Vikings be replaced by three Viscounts. With the Flight temporarily at Northolt, whilst its Benson hangar was being rennovated, discussions concerning new equipment went ahead bringing sufficient confidence for Vickers to earmark Viscount airframes in production for VIP and VVIP completion. A firm commitment was awaited for eighteen months before official sanction was given for the Flight's new establishment to comprise one Viscount 700D, one VVIP Viking, a Heron and two Whirlwind helicopters. The problem ever facing the Flight was how to maintain value to set against the cost of capital equipment and maintenance over a long period. For Her Majesty to have made use of one of the finest airliners of its time would certainly have given that a prestigious boost, for which reason the purchase would have been sensible. The decision not to go ahead with the Viscount scheme, irrespective of the economics involved, cannot be concluded as wise.

September 1954 brought the Flight its first helicopter, a small Westland Dragonfly HC4-XF261, from CFS South Cerney. It was intended for temporary service but resided at Benson for four years. Sanction for the Queen's Flight to operate two VVIP helicopters was given in July 1954 and the first royal helicopter journey came on 6 September 1954 when Prince Philip flew in the Dragonfly from Buckingham Palace to Shinfield. Although many members of the Royal Family used XF261, it mostly carried Prince Philip who, in 1955, qualified as a helicopter pilot. His Heron C3, XH375, joined the Flight on 18 May 1955. Upon its highly burnished finish it wore an Edinburgh Green cheat line in keeping with its pilot's title. Both Devon and Heron were placed at White Waltham until July 1955 when they moved to Benson.

Summer 1955 saw Prince Philip making use of a naval Whirlwind 22, the Dragonfly being switched to route and landing area survey. Satisfied of the value of helicopters, the Air Council agreed to Whirlwinds being added to the Flight's establishment the following spring. Various delays arose and not until July 1958 was a contract for two VVIP Whirlwind 8s placed, for 1959 delivery. Meanwhile a Whirlwind 4 replaced the small Dragonfly. Trouble with the Alvis Leonides Major engine which powered the Whirlwind delayed the Mk 8s Benson debut until October 1959. Not until 23 September 1960 did the new Whirlwind make its first Royal passenger flight, from Kensington Palace to Papworth.

Replacements for the Vikings were ordered in April 1956 in the form of two Heron C4s. Two years later they came into use, Prince Philip's Heron along with Vikings VL233 and VL246 having long borne their royal role. Not until 22 April 1958 did the last Viking flight take place, then the two new Herons arrived within a few days.

Subsequently the Royal Herons — bright red overall from 1960 — were used in many distant parts of the world. Their payload/range characteristics were limited and for the Royal Tour of India and the Himalayas, two Dakotas (KN452, previously used by the AOC Malta and KN645, once the transport of Field Marshal Montgomery) were acquired. Nevertheless, a fourth Heron joined the Flight in

Benson's Royal helicopters include Wessex XV733.

June 1961 and was used during Princess Alexander's tour of the Far East, despite dissatisfaction with the Heron's overall performance.

In March 1964 the first of two Gnome turbo-engined Whirlwind 12s to replace the Mk 8s came into use at Benson as agreement was reached to replace the Herons by Andovers. The first two of these came into the Flight in July-August 1964.

Prince Philip flew to the North Sea rig, *Sea Quest*, in a 72 Squadron Wessex during June 1967 as consideration was being given to the Flight using such aircraft. HRH Queen Elizabeth, the Queen Mother, came to be quoted as saying that 'the chopper' had changed

Briefly part of the Queen's Flight was this Beagle Basset XS770.

her life as much as it did Anne Boleyn's, but whether the use of helicopters would continue came into doubt on 7 December 1967 when Whirlwind *XL487* crashed as a result of a rotor shaft snapping. Air Commodore J. H. L. Blount, Captain of the Queen's Flight, was among those killed and all Whirlwinds were promptly grounded pending a court of enquiry. Not until the end of March 1968 did the Queen's Flight resume helicopter flying.

The last Royal Heron, *XM296*, left on 25 June 1968 after ten years service and an accumulation of 4,310 flying hours. Several Wessex helicopters were used before mid-1969. The VVIP Wessex HCC4's first task was to carry the Prince of Wales to his Investiture at Caernarvon. Later that year a Basset was placed at Benson for the Prince's use and also for general communications flying. It remained at Benson until 16 September 1971 when it was despatched to 32 Squadron, Northolt.

January 1983 saw the arrival from Brize Norton of seven Andover E.3/3A of No 115 Squadron whose tasks are radar calibration and as a secondary employment casualty evacuation. The squadron replaced the Wessex helicopters of 72 Squadron which moved to Aldergrove, Northern Ireland.

Having the Andover E.3s here meant that servicing of these and the three used by the Queen's Flight could be done conveniently. The Andover CC Mk 2 was first used for an overseas tour in October 1964 when Prince Philip toured Mexico and the Caribbean. Over the next two years the Andovers were extensively used during Royal tours to Africa, the Middle and Far East, North America and the Caribbean as well as within Europe. A third Andover was added to the Flight in December 1967 and this signalled the retirement of the Heron which type managed 941 Royal flights flying two million miles.

The Andovers *XS789*, *XS790* and *XS793*, have been very active in their Royal Flight days, being seen in many parts of the world. In 1972 they changed their colours, after the original 'alclad' skin of the exposed aluminium underbody of the aircraft was showing signs of corrosion caused by continual polishing! A Union Flag was applied to the tails of the aircraft in December 1973.

On 23 April 1986 *ZE700*, the first of two

Benson has been the home of the Andovers of the Queen's Flight since 1964. XS790 was conveying the Royal party to the RAF 50th Anniversary Display at Abingdon when photographed on 14 June 1968.

Above *Summer 1986 saw the celebration of the 50th Anniversary of a Royal Flight and the arrival for The Queen's Flight of two BAe 146 CC Mk 2s. The first example, ZE700, was handed over The Queen's Flight on 23 April 1986. (BAe.)*

Below *The Royal Compartment aboard ZE700. (BAe.)*

BAe 146-100 four-engined jets known to the RAF as the BAe 146 CC Mk 2, was handed over to the Royal Flight. A second example, *ZE701*, followed in late June at which time the Flight was about to celebrate its 50th Anniversary. Between June and September 1983 the RAF evaluated two BAe 146s and after 800 hours trials recommended two aircraft of the type serve with the Royal Flight. As a result two Andovers were retired to 32 Squadron, the remaining aircraft being retained for back-up purposes.

The role of the Queen's Flight, whose aircraft are based at Benson and fly from there to other airfields for the commencement of Royal journeys, is primarily to provide air transport for the Queen, Members of the Royal Family, the Prime Minister, certain senior Ministers, the Chief of Staff and their foreign equivalents visiting the United Kingdom who may also use the aircraft if one is available. Just how valuable that task may be for advertising British aircraft is only too clear, raising yet again the question of 'why did the Flight not receive the …'?

Compared with the Andover the BAe 146 can carry twice the load and twenty VIP passengers against twelve previously. It can fly nearly twice as fast — 400 knots against 230 knots — and almost twice as far again — 1,900 miles against 1,000 miles. The Queen will have a more comfortable ride since the BAe 146 can fly at 30,000 ft to avoid bad weather. Its four engines confer higher safety levels, and its short field performance rivals the Andover's exceeding it by confering greater safety when taking off from high altitudes and in high temperatures. The BAe 146 carried their Royal Highnesses the Duke and Duchess of York to the Azores for their honeymoon, and the Queen and Prince Philip during the Royal tour of China in 1986.

Of all the airfields in central England, Benson is one of the most aesthetically sited. In its PR days a posting here was not universally popular. The work was hard and tedious, the hours long and the value of achievement largely unrealized as it was created. One may drive through this camp, view its domestic site, typical in design, while having to the north a splendid view over conventionally flat-roofed buildings of the 1930s beyond which, placed lower, are the hangars. It is easy to imagine the great days of the blue Spits and Mossies. Close your eyes; can you hear two fast-revving Merlins on a thick, misty day coming ever closer? Ah, memories of John Merifield, and of Victor and Boris racing home from Paris, all carrying a precious cargo able to change history. Perhaps things haven't changed all that much at Benson?

Bicester

SP595245. 1½ miles NE of Bicester town, by the A421

Leaving Bicester on the Buckingham Road one immediately sees a long-established military site where a 1934 control tower in good condition is one of the last in Britain. Bicester of the 1980s occupies Caller's Field upon which, in 1916, British and Canadian engineers — assisted by Chinese and Portuguese workers and press-ganged German POWS — began to construct a Training Depot Station in Southern Army Command. Americans joined in, providing an electric power station, for a while the only one in the district.

The camp came into use late in 1917. In January 1918, 118 Squadron RFC mobilized here and remained until November 1918. No 44 Training Depot Station arrived at the start of October 1918. Between mid-February 1919 and September of that year, No 2 Squadron resided at Bicester and was replaced on 19 September 1919 by 5 Squadron's Bristol Fighters, freshly returned from France and disbanded on 20 January 1920. Bicester closed in March 1920.

Following the 1924 decision to site bomber squadrons in the Oxford area, resurrection of RAF Bicester commenced in 1925. Buildings on the technical site were placed within a pentagonal area, one hangar being on the southwest side and another on the south-east. An early layout provided for up to four more, with the original being to pattern 1154/27. A special feature was a railway

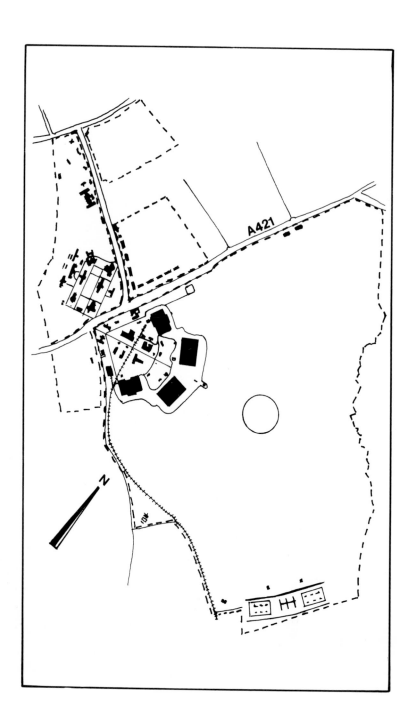

A421

link leading to the Main Stores (978/25), close to which were the Motor Transport (MT) sheds and an engine test house (702/26). Bicester's circular 30,000 gallon elevated water tank (1178/25) supplemented a 100,000 gallon reservoir. The present guardhouse retains much of the original (959/25). Provision for 192 seats was made in the Airmen's Dining Room, modified in 1925 and 1933 from its 1923 style. Original Airmen's Barrack Blocks were Type E, based on 1922-23 designs and each holding three NCOs and eighty men. Behind the 1924-25 SHQ building was the camera obscura. On the airfield was a concrete compass swinging platform with a diameter of 50 ft.

The new camp opened in January 1928 and Hawker Horsleys of No 100 Squadron winged in from Spitalgate, leaving in November 1930 for Donibristle. No 33 Squadron's Hawker Harts arrived

Left *Bicester in January, 1939. The technical site lies to the east of the Buckingham road; the domestic area to west. To the east of the main road, into the technical site, lies first the guardhouse (959/25) then stores and workshops. SHQ faces the guardhouse to the east of which is the MT section. The armoury lies alongside. From north to south, the first two aircraft sheds are Type 'C' 1410-12/35 and 1154/27 and the other similar to that first within the arc. The watch tower Type 1959/34 stands at the apex of the apron. Across the landing ground lies the weapons dump. In the centre of the landing ground is a 4 ft wide chalk circle, 150 yd in diameter. This is a landing circle which marks the airfield clearly. Note the railway line leading to the stores, a feature of a number of airfields laid down in the 1920s.*

Below *Bicester was home for 33 Squadron's Hawker Harts in the early 1930s.*

Boulton & Paul Overstrand K4561 resting between Bicester's hangars, Type 'A' to the right, Type 'C' left.

on 4 November 1930. They had a cherished place in RAF history when at Eastchurch in February 1930, they were the first to join a squadron. No 33 remained at Bicester, and in the limelight until the end of November 1934. It was replaced on 4 December 1934 by the only Sidestrand squadron, No 101. Between October 1935 and July 1936 Overstrands replaced them, the first

Product of the expansion period of the 1930s, the gracious Officer's Mess at Bicester, and now Cherwell House, a nursing home.

example, *K4547*, arriving on 14 October 1935. These were the first RAF bombers with enclosed power-operated turrets.

Within the 1930's Expansion Scheme, Bicester had a major face lift. Two 'C' Type hangers (1581/35, 2392/37) were constructed, supplementing the older ones, all of which remain. Barrack blocks of the Extended E Type (2489/37), accommodating one NCO and 96 men, were added, as was the Watch Office and Tower (1959/34). East of the playing fields stands the Officer's Mess. By the start of 1939, nine barrack blocks had been built, nine married quarters units for airmen and another six for officers. By that time Bicester had seen plenty of the RAF's expansion programme.

The first new squadron was No 48 (General Reconnaissance) Squadron which formed on 25 November 1935 and moved to Manston in mid-December. Bicester joined the Western Area on 1 April 1936 and 3 Group on 30 April 1936. Transfer to 1 Group became effective on 17 August 1936. Station Headquarters was established on 21 September 1936 to run Bicester more effectively.

No 144 Squadron formed from C Flight 101 Squadron on 11 January 1937, and left for Hemswell on 8 February 1937. No 90 Squadron, was temporarily equipped with Hinds until May 1937 when the Blenheim 1s arrived. No 101 Squadron had to wait until June 1938 for Blenheims.

The Munich crisis plunged the station into a high state of readiness giving a taste of 2 Group. For much of the war, Bicester was to feed crews into that courageous body. Maybe sampling of 2 Group's high camaraderie encouraged the moves of 90 and 101 Squadrons on 9 May 1939, to 2 Group's station at West Raynham. Two squadrons of Fairey Battles of 1 Group, Nos 12 and 142 then came from Andover, as part of Field Force France. Both squadrons left Bicester to become part of the AASF on 2 September 1939.

Once at war, the station again courted 2 Group with the arrival, on 12 September 1939, of Nos 104 and 108 Blenheim Squadrons, supplemented by Ansons to form No 2 Group Pool and under 6

Group's control. Pilots and observers were recruited from flying training schools, observer schools and the RAFVR. Air gunners came from 2 Group squadrons' ground crews. Although specialized aircrew, they retained airmen ranks and, even more meanly, their old rates of pay. Training a Blenheim crew took six months.

Bicester's personnel had a morale booster on 25 October 1939. Vehicles from Handley Page works at Cricklewood had conveyed a secret bomber here. In the hangar by Launton Road the Halifax prototype, *L7244*, was erected and, on 25 October 1939, first flew. After a few flights it left for Boscombe Down.

Bicester's two squadrons merged to form No 13 OTU on 8 April 1940. Then training the Blenheim crews increased to meet crippling losses during the French campaign. King George VI visited the station on 19 July 1940, and many whom he met were to die in the awful punishment 2 Group sustained during the following fourteen months. On 22 July 1940 control of 13 OTU passed to 7 Group.

Bicester's satellite at Weston-on-the-Green now came into use for night flying which also started at Hinton-in-the-Hedges in November. A dummy airfield at Grendon Underwood was ready to attract enemy bombs. That month Lewis gunners manning a Bicester defence post claimed hits on passing Ju 88 L1+LS which came down at Blewbury, Berkshire.

In its first year 13 OTU trained 217 pilots, 240 observers and 273 air gunners. The flying hours totalled 26,670. Demand for Blenheim crews increased for home and overseas squadrons and 2 Group's merciless anti-shipping campaign. From October 1941, Blenheim crews were trained at 13 OTU mainly to meet Middle East needs. The OTU's second year produced 32,718 flying hours and 297 complete crews, 121 of them going overseas. Bicester's bombers came nearest to participating in offensive action when they flew air/sea rescue searches after the '1,000 bomber' raids. From July 1942 a higher proportion of its output proceeded to further training

For part of the war, crews for the squadrons of No 2 (Bomber) Group were Bicester trained. Shown are Blenheim IVs of 13 OTU. R3607 (nearest) flew many operational sorties with Nos 57, 59, 40 and 18 Squadrons, joined 13 OTU in June 1941 and crashed on 13 March 1942.

and heavy bomber squadrons because of single pilot manning of new bombers.

There were changes, too, in the station's satellites. Finmere served from 31 July 1942 to 28 November 1942 and Turweston from 1 October 1942 to 28 November 1942, and again in mid-1943. On 20 November 1942, No 1551 BAT Flight formed from the Blind Approach Calibration Flight and used four Ansons, three Oxfords and two Masters. On 15 April 1943 this Flight became part of the Signals Development Unit.

During Operation *Torch*, the Blenheim V at last went into battle, crews being drawn from 13 OTU. Replacement aircraft became urgently needed in Africa and could only be flown there, and so No 307 Ferry Training Unit formed at Bicester and, from 24 December 1942, had the task of training thirty ferry crews for which seven Blenheim Vs were made available.

On the afternoon of 5 April 1943, five Blenheims of 13 OTU flew a North Sea ASR sweep, the last such operation. By April 1943 there were only twelve crews per course. Training was to switch to producing Boston and Mitchell crews who flew at the satellites because these aircraft needed hard runways.

On 1 June 1943, 13 OTU left Bomber Command and joined 70 Group Fighter Command, in preparation for the training of 2 TAF crews. Nevertheless, the OTU continued to rely upon Blenheims — mainly dual control Mk Vs — for operational conversion. Some Spitfires arrived for fighter affiliation training before control of the unit passed to 9 Group on 1 November 1943. Bicester then received specialized units of 84 and 85 Groups 2 TAF training for their roles, and became the Forward Equipment Unit for both Groups. All 13 OTU's Blenheim flying ceased on 25 February 1944, the last short-nosed Blenheim 1 leaving Bicester three days later.

Bicester's backing to 2TAF became increasingly apparent following D-Day and conflicted with the running of a busy OTU. When 38 Group vacated Harwell in mid-October 1944, 13 OTU took over that station which became its main base. Thereafter Bicester served almost exclusively as a 'non-flying' station. The Forward Equipment Unit of 85 Group became 246 MU on 1 January 1945 and transferred to 40 Group, Maintenance Command. It became a transit centre for despatch of equipment to 2 TAF on the Continent, and assembly point for its vehicles — in particular those radio equipped — as well as Command Centre for aero engines and vehicle spares. BAFO was supplied until September 1945, then the station served as a motor transport depot. Headquarters 40 Group arrived from Andover during February 1947, staying until 1961.

Return to flying came during the brief stay of the Beam Approach Calibration Flight which arrived in July 1947.

No 246 MU disbanded on 1 April 1949, then a parachute packing and servicing unit moved in. Between 3 September 1951 and 30 January 1954 the Civilian Supplies Technical Officers' School functioned here. No 71 MU opened as a 43 Group lodger unit on 15 December 1953, repair, salvage and transport Service aircraft involved in flying accidents occurring south of the line roughly joining Aberdovey to the Wash. Assistance was also rendered to incidents involving civilian aircraft. Within 71 MU were a bomb disposal flight and the Historic Aircraft Exhibition Flight which restored the famous Lancaster in the RAF Museum.

Chipmunks of Oxford University Air Squadron moved into Bicester in 1959 and remained until September 1975. As part of the Strategic Reserve, No 5 Light Anti-Aircraft Wing formed here in 1967 and included No 2 Light Anti-Aircraft Squadron which had been in Malaysia defending RAF bases during the Indonesian confrontation. The Wing disbanded in 1970, by which time the RAF Gliding and Soaring Association had been on the station for seven years, and continues to make use of it.

Bicester closed as an active station on 31 March 1976 and was placed under Abingdon's control for care and maintenance. Transfer to the Army Department followed on 20 May 1976. Unexpectedly, the barracks became RAF Bicester again on 22 November 1978 and recently the station (parts of which have been disposed of) has been used as a storage site by the Americans. An adventure school is also run here.

Bicester's remaining buildings span over fifty years of service. Thus the station is of particular architectural interest. What is surprising in view of its age is that Bicester, in over half a century, has never despatched one offensive sortie.

An unusual sight in Britain were Beverleys of 84 Squadron which ended their days at Bicester.

Brize Norton

SP295060. 6 miles SW of Witney

With effortless delight, XR806 climbed away from Brize Norton's 10,000 ft runway. The captain muttered something about this '... noise abatement procedure'. Few joys in the jet world can remotely equal being 'up front' in a VC10. It looks good, it feels good, it is good — just a superlative aeroplane.

Brize Norton is home for the RAF's VC10. From here the remains of the strategic reserve can be deployed and aircraft making long duration sorties can be refuelled in flight. It is also the place from which important people fly, or obtain their aeroplanes — and they fly RAF in the full knowledge that its 'airline' has an outstanding safety record. Nice, too, when one leans out to see a comforting roundel in place of the nasty, cheap colours of civilian competitors!

It's impossible to miss Brize Norton as it sprawls across a flat section of Oxfordshire. At times the water table must be high, but apparently the area has never been flooded. Naming the station posed a problem for it lies mainly within the Carterton boundary, a name too reminis- cent of Cardington to be suitable. So Brize Norton was chosen when building started in 1935. Exceptional was the completion of five 'C' Type hangars, planned for many stations but rarely built. It was incomplete, but 2 Flying Training School nevertheless moved in on 13 August 1937. The school brought a mixture of Hawker Harts, the first of which had been received in April 1935, Audaxes, first received in May 1936, and Hawker Furies to hold the line until monoplanes arrived. First to come, on 22 February 1938, was an Airspeed Oxford. Four more arrived in March, one in April after which they trickled into use, allowing realistic pilot training. A divorced group of buildings was erected, a motley collection, including 'Lamella' and Type D hangars, to house No 6 Maintenance Unit in the airfield's south-east corner. A 41 Group unit, it opened on 10 October 1938, receiving its first two aircraft, Saro Cloud amphibians, on 30 January 1939.

The most audible change descended upon 2 SFTS in March 1939 when ten Harvard 1s arrived. Another thirteen came in June to further torment the populace and two more in July 1939. Close by, 6 MU placed thirteen in storage

Quite incomparable in its class, VC 10 C Mk 1 XV107 climbs away from Brize Norton.

Top *One of the busiest units in wartime Oxfordshire was No 6 MU whose 'D' Type hangars remain prominent in the south-eastern area of Brize Norton.*

Above *Curious mound-like hangars of the Lamella type were available for aircraft storage.*

that month. By the time war started more Oxfords were with the FTS. Blenheims of 101 Squadron scattered here and at Weston-on-the-Green which became Brize Norton's active satellite. 6 MU early in the war supplied Gladiators to Finland and Blenheims to Yugoslavia.

The fall of France sent shudders of anxiety throughout the area. Middle Wallop, needed for fighter squadrons, had its 15 SFTS moved, Oxfords and Harvards comprising half the Intermediate Training

Harvard 1s of 2 SFTS at Brize Norton, summer 1940. (IWM.)

A Whitley V glider tug lands over Horsa gliders of Brize Norton's HGCU. (IWM.)

Squadron being lodged at Brize Norton from 11 June while awaiting the availability of Kidlington. HQ 15 SFTS came along too, prior to acquiring a palatial residence, Oldner House at Chipping Norton, into which a move was made on 10 July 1940.

Risk of enemy interference with flying training was proven on 28 July 1940 when a 2 SFTS Oxford was shot down over Akeman Street. That the enemy really meant business was disastrously obvious when, on the afternoon of Friday 16 August two Ju 88s wrought tremendous havoc at the station. Training aircraft had been hangared for protection

A Horsa trainer being prepared for attachment to a Whitley tug. Such gliders were brightly painted, with black and yellow stripes on their under surfaces. (IWM.)

against the elements, but no longer. Most of the serviceable Oxfords were dispersed, some at Akeman Street, others at Southrop, and 15 SFTS left on 19 August. Although Brize Norton was attacked three more times, it suffered little further damage.

Throughout 1941, 2 SFTS trained RAF pilots while 6 MU handled a multiplicity of aircraft types. Most common were Blenheims, Hampdens, Hurricanes, Spitfires and Fairey Battles which, no longer fighting machines, languished long at Brize Norton.

November 1941, when the first Empire Air Training Scheme pilots arrived for acclimatization flying, also saw the formation here of 25 Blind Approach Training Flight. It became 1525 BAT Flight on 18 February 1942 and remained here until 13 July 1942. On 14 March 1942, 2 SFTS had become 2 (P) AFU. Too many such units existed by the summer and, on 14 July, the organization closed.

Next day Brize Norton acquired a unique role with the arrival of the recently formed Heavy Glider Conversion Unit from Shrewton. The station now became the training centre where Army glider pilots would come to learn how to handle the hefty Horsa, intended backbone of

the airborne forces. 6 MU was to erect many Horsas over the next three years. After flight testing they were locally used or towed to dispersal sites on bomber bases.

Trainee pilots came from Glider Training Schools, course strength being 62 pupils. Aircraft establishment was set at 56 Horsas and 34 Whitley V glider tugs. Glider flying was no simple affair. It took time to marshal the glider, attach the tow rope and position the tug. Accidents were frequent; night training difficult. On 21 October 1942 a Glider Instructors' School formed, staying until February 1944 when it moved to North Luffenham.

With very many aircraft in store, 6 MU acquired the use of 34 Satellite Landing Ground Woburn in November 1941, relinquished in favour of No 28 SLG Barton Abbey on 8 February 1943, a site taken from 39 MU Colerne. Woburn was then handed to 8 MU, Little Rissington. No 22 SLG Barnsley Park was also used.

Whitley/Horsa combinations were intractable affairs with a wide turning circle. Already the Central Gliding Area contained ample tugs and Hotspurs on daily rounds, so cross country routes were awarded to the Heavy Glider Conversion Unit whose Whitleys and Horsas

paraded widely as single combinations well spaced. Between 10 February and 20 April 1943, flying also took place from Grove while Brize Norton's runways were re-surfaced. The primary task of the HGCU was to train sufficient Horsa pilots for the Sicilian landing. Then it switched to the main task — training for the landings in Europe.

Sufficient done, the HGCU was reduced in strength to forty Whitley Vs and 36 Horsas, and moved to North Luffenham in March 1944. Brize Norton switched to an operational role in 38 Group. A new SHQ was set up on 13 March 1944 and within hours Albemarles of 296 and 297 Squadrons arrived. Then they fetched their Horsas from dispersal sites, ready for the assault on Normandy. On 20 March 1944, operational training commenced in earnest with the dropping of paratroops, and towing and releasing gliders accurately.

On the night of 5–6 June 1944, eighteen Albemarles drawn from both squadrons carried the 5th Parachute Brigade to LZ 'N', a position by the river Orne in Normandy where a landing ground was fast prepared for seventeen Horsas towed out of Brize Norton. Another two, brought by 297 Squadron, landed by the Merville coastal gun site. During the early evening of 6 June, forty Horsas were towed across the Channel from Brize

Norton, and carried part of the 6th Airborne Division lifted during Operation *Mallard*.

Albemarle squadrons then flew supply dropping sorties over France, while maintaining their glider towing skill. Because of their limited range and possibilities of engine overheating during the next major operation, Brize Norton's Albemarles flew to Manston on 15 September 1944. From there they operated twice, towing gliders to Arnhem during Operation *Market* before returning to Brize Norton. Both squadrons were then to convert to Stirling IVs and, on 29–30 September, left for Earl's Colne taking with them 94 Horsas.

Arnhem's high casualty rate meant training more glider pilots for another Rhine crossing attempt. The HGCU's Whitleys and Horsas returned from North Luffenham on 15 October 1944. Sufficient glider pilots could not be trained by one unit, therefore other units formed. Brize Norton becoming No 21 HGCU. Some American Waco Hadrians were added to its strength in November. An Instructors' School which arrived in October remained until December 1945.

With the increase in activity, 6 MU repossessed Woburn SLG where it placed surplus Stirlings. 21 HGCU began re-arming with Albemarles in January 1945 and by February enough glider

Left   *Armstrong-Whitworth Albemarles were a common sight over Oxfordshire in 1943-44. MkII P5-S: V1823 of 297 Squadron based at Brize Norton took part in both operational glider tows during the D-Day landings on 6 June 1944 and in the Arnhem landings on 17 September 1944, flying from Manston.*

Right *Many German aircraft were handled postwar by 6 MU Brize Norton, including this Arado Ar 234B-2 jet.*

pilots were ready for another Rhine assault. Training continued against possible Far East needs.

As Europe fêted the end of hostilities, the few aircraft enthusiasts of those days were about to enjoy unforgettable moments. Over the following few weeks some 200 captured enemy aircraft were brought to Britain for detailed examination or usefully employed as temporary transports. What would the morrow bring, one asked, and to where were they being taken? Mainly to Farnborough, but the support organization was provided by 6 MU. Many German aircraft came to Britain from Schleswigland, and once here they shuttled between Royal Aircraft Establishment and 6 MU, occasionally venturing further afield.

Brize Norton's first captive was, satisfyingly, a Ju 88 which landed on 10 May 1945. Many exciting shapes followed, among them the Focke-Wulf Ta *152H-150168* which came from RAE on 18 August and stayed until 22 October. Heinkel *219A-7* Air Min 20 came on 21 August and was followed by another, ten days later. 30 June brought Arado *Ar234B-140008* from Farnborough and a Heinkel 162 touched down on 2 August. An Me 410 and '6158', one of the two Dornier 217Ms brought for examination, were among the aircraft here by the end of 1945. 'Why did not someone save them?' You may well ask. In those days conservation was unknown, and most weathered away or were dismembered in the late 1940s.

Halifaxes replaced the station's Albemarle tugs before 21 HGCU left for Elsham Wolds in late December 1945. Brize Norton then joined Transport Command — apart from 6 MU. The School of Flight Efficiency and Transport Command Development Unit arrived from Harwell, for which reason Hampstead Norris and Finmere came under Brize Norton's control.

TCDU's principle task was development of airborne delivery of mixed loads. It employed Dakotas, Halifaxes, Hamilcars, Horsas, Stirlings, Yorks and a few Hoverfly helicopters. Later it conducted glider towing trials of the Hastings and Valetta. In May 1946 the Army Airborne Trials and Development Unit arrived, the activity here attracting American interest and the exotic sight of a Fairchild C-82 Packet towing a Horsa.

On 5 September 1946, Halifax A IXs of 297 Squadron arrived and stayed until August 1947. September 1946 also brought a Douglas C-54 automatically flown here from America, whilst 6 MU was disposing of many aircraft, in particular Spitfires. In January 1948 the MU received its first Meteors. TCDU left for Abingdon on 30 June 1949 and on 4 July

Here, a Ju 52 3/m awaits its journey to 6 MU.

Brize Norton came under 21 Group Training Command. A swarm of Harvards again settled, this time belonging to the Examining Wing of Central Flying School. They were joined in mid-August by Mosquito T.3s and 6s of 204 AFS. Once more the emphasis shifted to training, Fairford serving as the Relief Landing Ground. CFS remained until 16 May 1950, and the Mosquitoes left for Swinderby early in June. By then the station was being administered by 23 Group, but not for long. Just before the trainers left, news broke of alien times ahead. Bomber Command seized Brize Norton on 1 June 1950 on behalf of the United States Strategic Air Command.

Embryo plans for SAC B-29 bases had existed since 1946, and Russian intransigence over Berlin forced them to be enacted. Temporary bases lay along and ahead of the eastern fighter belt whereas the Americans naturally wanted bases to its rear. Final site selection was made in May 1950, Fairford, Greenham Common, Upper Heyford and Brize Norton being chosen. Each needed at least a 9,000 ft runway, revised dispersals and alert

B-47B 51-2261 of the 320th Bomb Wing, one of many US Strategic Air Command Stratojets operated from Brize Norton.

areas — and of course very secure weapons dumps. On 7 June 1950 the first Americans moved here from Marham, freeing the latter for RAF B-29s. The official hand over to the USAF took place on 16 April 1951, but not until 27 June 1952 did the first deployment of American bombers take place and spectacular it was, for it involved 21 giant B-36D and B-36Fs from the three squadrons of the 11th Bomb Wing (H), Carswell AFB. They spent fifteen days at Brize Norton.

Reorganization of facilities led to the 7503rd Strategic Wing supervizing running of the SAC base. Regular SAC rotational TDYs commenced with the

It was impossible to mistake a Convair B-36. Its colossal size, and the tremendous din it created in slowly passing overhead combined to produce one of the most spectacular aviation sights of all time. Both the 7th and 11th Bomb Wings detached B-36Ds and Fs to Brize Norton. (Mitch Mayborn.)

arrival in December 1952 of B-29s of the 301st BW (M). In March 1953, 65 Squadron, 43rd BW (M), flying B-50As, replaced the 301st, making simultaneous use of four UK bases and staying longer than usual whilst plans were prepared to station B-47s in Britain.

Following the 43rd's return to America in June, there was a break before Brize Norton received, during the evening of 4 September 1953, the first of many B-47 Stratojets based here. This initial rotation brought two squadrons of the 305th BW (M) from Limestone AFB, Maine. Replacement came in the form of the 22nd BW (M) which placed one of its B-47B squadrons here. Subsequent B-47s at the base were of the B-47E variety before summer 1954 brought more B-47Bs, this time of the 320th BW (M) which were followed by B-47Es of the 43rd BW (M).

In December 1954 the base's first tanker squadron, the 321st Air Refuelling Squadron using KC-97Gs, moved in. Their aircraft, unusually, had their 'last three' boldly displayed on their fins. By contrast the following KC-97Gs of the 310th ARS identified themselves merely by green fin tips. It was the 40th BW (M) that came next, again using KC-97Gs. They left in September 1955, flying home via Goose Bay to Smoky Hill.

Brize Norton then underwent runway repairs before reopening in July 1956. Limited use was subsequently made by B-47s of the 307th BW (M), and in January 1957 the 384th BW (M) placed B-47Es here. It was during their stay that, on 16 January 1957, the first Boeing B-52B to land in Britain (*3395 — City of Turlock of the 93 BW (H)*) touched down after a flight from Castle AFB California.

When the 380th BW (M) arrived in April 1957 it placed its three B-47E squadrons here and after it left, runway repairs again were undertaken. Some B-47s of the 68th Bomb Wing came at the start of 1958 and were then replaced by a squadron of the 100th BW (M).

On 28 March 1958 came the debut of another new type to the base when the first Boeing KC-135 tanker to visit Britain landed. Two more came on 27 June,

notching up record speed crossings during flights from New York. These 'flying gas stations' were welcome arrivals, unlike a B-47E on 28 February 1958. Shortly after taking off from Greenham Common it developed engine trouble and both of its long range tanks were immediately jettisoned. One bounced onto a hangar at Greenham setting it on fire, the other fell onto a B-47 which exploded. In the ensuing panic the Stratojet landed at Brize Norton. Fortunately, nuclear stores were not involved.

April 1958 brought six B-52Ds of the 92nd BW (H) to participate in the annual Anglo-American bombing competition. They came to a relatively empty base for, after the 100th had vacated it earlier in the month, new policy came into enactment. Only a handful of B-47s would now be at 'Brize' at any one time, their three-week stay replacing the previous 90-day temporary duty rotation. This 'Reflex Alert' meant more flexibility and less vulnerability. Sometimes as few as nine aircraft formed the detachment. For company they had, for varying periods, detachments of the 55th and 98th Stratetic Reconnaisance Wings, flying reconnaisance variants of the RB-47. Also based at Brize Norton early in 1959 was one of the little seen TB-47s. When the 38th BW (M) was in Britain (late 1959) it deployed 11 B-47s at Brize Norton along with KC-97Gs.

Varied detachments continued into the early 1960s including the first involving the basing of KC-135s here. More excitement was generated when, in January 1964, a Convair B-58 Hustler, the world's first supersonic bomber and of the 43rd BW, Carswell AFB, Texas, flew in. A few more followed but never more than a handful. B-47s continued to come despite their age, although there was now a gradual swing to Inter-Continental Ballistic Missiles for Strategic Air Command and towards American-based B-52s.

On 1 April 1965, Brize Norton returned to the RAF, after an interesting period to which it had attracted unusual American types such as U-2s (Gary Powers being involved), RB-47s and ERB-47s with all manner of intelligence capabilities. When

Brize Norton's giant hangar was built to accommodate Belfasts and VC10s. (Via Bruce Robertson.)

B-47E, *53-1884*, of the 380th BW (M) left on 3 April 1965, an era ended.

SAC vacated Brize Norton as Britain's transport force, strategic and tactical, was expanding. Forthcoming use of large aircraft made it essential that a base in addition to Lyneham be brought into use for the Belfast and VC10 fleets. The choice fell upon Brize Norton, for its good facilities and strategic siting. Cargo and passenger terminals were needed, also additional housing and suitable aircraft maintenance facilities. Among the latter was a need for a hangar large enough to house half a dozen aircraft of the Belfast/ VC10 size. This, the Brize Norton 'Canti-lever' MPBW Lacon 7203/64N, is an amazing 1,039 ft 6 in long and 193 ft 6 in wide. The height of the ceiling is 52 ft 5½ in rising to 88 ft 2 in at the top of the ridge. Within the structure are eleven bays alternately of 91 ft or 80 ft 6 in width. When completed in June 1967 it was the largest cantilever structure in western Europe, and cost nearly £2,000,000.

Despite the intensity of the work, the station was not ready in time to house the Belfast and VC10 squadrons which instead commenced operations from Lyneham and Fairford. It was mid-1967 when 10 and 53 Squadrons moved in. The demise of Transport Command

Inside the hangar, three VC 10s and two Belfasts. Nearest is VC 10 'David Lord VC'. (BAe.)

AIR   SUPPORT   COMMAND

Belfasts of 53 Squadron such as XR365 'Hector' were retired and in civilian hands before the South Atlantic campaign, yet they were also used.

came on 1 August, and it then became Air Support Command. VC10s of 10 Squadron were then working the trunk route to Hong Kong and supporting British commitments throughout the world, leaving the transportation of heavy items to 53 Squadron's Belfasts.

As soon as the Hercules fleet reached intended strength at Lyneham, both Britannia squadrons, Nos 99 and 511, moved to Brize Norton. 'Brits' performed excellently and were useful on account of their good field performance. The station was much in the news in the

During the latter period of their RAF service Bristol Britannias like Mk 2 XN404 'Canopus' were based at Brize Norton.

summer of 1974 when its transports lifted over 7,500 Service and civilian personnel in rapid time when trouble flared in Cyprus.

Not long after, the future for the large aircraft abruptly became bleak with a decision to phase out Britannias and Belfasts. The run down of the former force commenced in April 1975 and of the latter in June 1976. The removal of the Belfast could not have come at a worse time. Serious problems with some of the Hercules meant replacement of spars. Only the Belfast could bring them to Britain by air and replacement parts continued to be flown using *XR366* into the autumn of 1976 and even after 53 Squadron disbanded on 14 September 1976. At the end of that year Brize Norton looked very empty.

Cottesmore, once in line for TSR-2, was now choice for the Tri-National Tornado Training Unit. Argosy E1s of 115 Squadron were therefore moved to Brize Norton where, in February 1978, the last Argosy was replaced by the Andover E1. Such aircraft had been at Brize Norton for some time in the hands of 240 Operational Conversion Unit which borrowed these and other transports from various squadrons.

In 1976, No 1 Parachute Training School arrived from Abingdon, a unit which attracts Hercules from Lyneham for paratroop practices at South Cerney and Weston-on-the-Green. No 38 Group Tactical Communications Wing is also based here, and the Joint Air Transport Establishment, the modern equivalent of Transport Command Development Unit. In recent years Brize Norton has been used for Concorde pilot training, and it

Each of 10 Squadron's VC 10s commemorates the name or names of RAF holders of the Victoria Cross, Donald Garland and Thomas Gray being honoured on this aircraft.

Modern airfield buildings are functional in the extreme, as this view of Brize Norton's terminal building shows. Many of those wounded during the Falklands conflict were flown to the apron in to foreground.

has served as a major diversion airfield.

Brize Norton of the 1980s differs much from the airfield in wartime days. Its 10,006 ft asphalt runway 08/26, load factor LCGII can accept virtually the weightiest of all aircraft so it is not surprising that Brize Norton is the chosen base for the RAF's heaviest ever aircraft, the TriStars.

It remains the home of No 10 Squadron's dozen VC10s which still visit many parts of the world carrying Royalty and VVIPs. Many times the VC10s have with little publicity contributed to major events.

Falklands conflict casualties came home in VC 10s, XR807 among them.

ZE696 seen taking off from Brize Norton. This was one of the two BAe 146s whose suitability for the Queen's Flight was assessed at Brize Norton.

At the end of 1979 when the cease-fire came to Rhodesia they airlifted to that country a large British contingent to monitor the event. They were much involved in the Falklands conflict, operating many runs to Ascension carrying personnel and urgent stores. From the war zone the VC10s brought home many of the most seriously wounded. Services are operated to Cyprus and Belize and support is given by these aircraft to exercises and troop movements. In a war situation 10 Squadron would serve in a battle support role.

Brize Norton now accommodates the RAF's five VC10 K2 tankers and four VC10 K3s (Super VC10s converted, the first entering service in February 1985) which equip 101 Squadron. The latter reformed here on 1 May 1984, and the earlier possibility that Vulcan tankers might be based here lapsed. To make way for the recent developments the Andover E3s of 115 Squadron moved to Benson in January 1983.

Crews for the transport aircraft continue to be trained by 241 OCU which borrows aircraft as needed. When consideration was given to assessing the suitability for the Queen's Flight of the BAe 146-100, 241 OCU handled the task using *ZD695 (G-OBAF)* and *ZD696 (G-SCHH)*, both of which have returned to civilian hands. No 1 Parachute Training School remains, responsible for training paratroopers as well as fielding the famous 'Falcons', the RAF's parachute team. JATE (the Joint Air Transport Establishment) continues to conduct trials and development of ideas for improving transport operations, and Brize Norton is now the base of No 19 Squadron, RAF Regiment, which is equipped with Rapier surface-to-air guided weapons. Its task is the defence of US bases in Britain. Thus, this is a very busy station whose activities began to take on more enormous proportions when the TriStars arrived.

It was June 1983 when two ex-British Airways TriStars commenced trooping flights from Brize Norton, giving the station a taste of what was involved in the handling and operation of wide-bodied jets with a capacity far in advance of

TriStar ZD948 was initially used purely as a transport aircraft which is why it retained its one-time British Airways colour scheme.

anything previously in Service hands. Merely taxying the newcomer around the perimeter track of some of the most sophisticated RAF airfields needs care, and the weight of the aircraft further restricts it when fairly heavily loaded. October 1983 saw RAF aircrew joining the flight crews of British Airways, then on 1 November 1983 216 Squadron reformed and soon applied its insignia to the tails of the TriStars. Eventually 216 Squadron will hold up to four of each TriStar type, the K1/K2 tanker and KC1 with special cargo facilities with probably a spare aircraft available. The first TriStar K1 arrived at Brize Norton for RAF service on 25 March 1986 to massively increase the RAFs in-flight refuelling capability allowing fighters to remain airborne for greatly increased periods. The later mixed load tanker-freighter TriStars will allow for operational flexibility and reinforcement capability which only the USAF possesses by way of its KC10

Extenders. Brize Norton's transports have changed quite a lot since the days of the Albemarle!

Broadwell

SP250065, 3½ miles S of Burford
Perhaps to the sound of a VC10, travel along the A361 Burford-Lechlade road. Within a few moments, fork left just beyond the Wild Life Park on to a road which crosses an open area. A few huts, the watch office and a distant Braithwaite water tower remain marking where RAF Broadwell once thrived.

A 70 Group opening up party arrived on 15 November 1943, and Transport Command took control on 24 January 1944. An advance party of 46 Group personnel arrived from Down Ampney on 2 February 1944 and, four days later, the first representatives of 512 and 575 Dakota squadrons came from Hendon. Aircraft and main parties arrived on 14

February 1944, bringing Horsa gliders.

Like other 46 Group stations Broadwell had a three-fold role: i) delivery of airborne forces and supplies, ii) transport runs to the Continent and iii) retrieval of wounded troops. To organize the ambulance service, elements of Nos 91, 92 and 93 Forward Staging Posts reached the station on 29 February 1944, by which time 220 commissioned and 1,400 non-commissioned men were stationed there.

On 4 April 1944, Broadwell took part in Exercise *Dreme*, its first major practice landing. This involved the night landing of troops of the 1st Air Landing Brigade lifted in 30 Dakotas supplied by the two squadrons. Then came a major 'navex' involving 35 aircraft, and glider tow practices were also flown. At dawn on 21 April 248 men parachuted from nineteen Dakotas in Exercise *Mush*. Rapid return to base, glider attachment and eighteen Dakotas with Horsas left within an hour. Dakota squadrons also undertook night training leaflet drops over France, four crews of each Broadwell squadron participating on 2 April 1944.

The Luftwaffe deposited three unexploded HEs on the southern extremity of the airfield on 23 April. Had the Luftwaffe dropped incendiary loads upon the wooden Horsa gliders ... Luckily, the potential of such a blow was not appreciated.

On 24 and 25 April both Dakota squadrons showered leaflets onto St Lô and Vire, despatching 21 effective night sorties. May brought a rapid increase in exercises. Exercise *Exeter*, watched by their Majesties King George VI and Queen Elizabeth, included dropping of paratroops at Netheravon where radio homing beacons were set up at the dropping zone to lead in thirty Dakotas from Broadwell to drop 300 troops of the 6th Airbrone Division. At the end of May spare gliders were towed away to Ramsbury by USAAF C-47s.

Tension rose quickly at the end of May for the invasion of the Continent was near. Orders were given to seal the station and impound all mail as from 14:00 on 2 June, for Broadwell was hosting over 1,000 troops for the Normandy landing. Upon receipt of the executive order on 5 June a final briefing for those taking part was arrang. d for 20:00. Fifty-nine crews attended, including six spare crews, for Operation *Tonga*. Present at the briefing was the AOC, 46 Group, who stressed the vital importance of the venture before the crews and troops boarded their aircraft.

Leading Broadwell's contingent was Wing Commander Coventry of 512 Squadron who took off at 23:14. His 32 aircraft were away in fifteen minutes, then came Wing Commander Jefferson with the first of 575 Squadron's crews. The whole force was airborne by 23:36, and the paradrop went well and without loss. On to the two dropping zones 952 troops had parachuted.

At 14:00 on 6 June crews of both Broadwell squadrons were briefed again, eighteen from 512 and nineteen from 575, for Operation *Mallard*. They were to tow loaded Horsa gliders to Normandy in daylight, protected by a massive fighter screen. Again all went well — until one aircraft had trouble which meant attaching its glider to a spare Dakota. All returned except for one which ditched in the Channel. Additional Dakotas took part the following night in Operation *Robroy*, a special operation during which they dropped supplies.

Commencement of Broadwell's third phase on 17 June set the tone for the rest of the war. At 06:00 fifteen Dakotas of 575 Squadron took off for Holmsley South taking aboard 191 RAF personnel and their kit. One Dakota became unserviceable leaving the others to make history by touching down at B5 landing strip (Camilly) the first Dakota squadron to land in France in force after D-Day. Landing was chancy and two damaged Dakotas had to be left there whilst the others hurried to B2 (Bazenville), there to retrieve 254 casualties who were back in England before mid-afternoon. This was the first huge input to the Air Ambulance Pool.

Apart from retrieving wounded, Dakotas of both squadrons aided squadron moves, then returned with casualties,

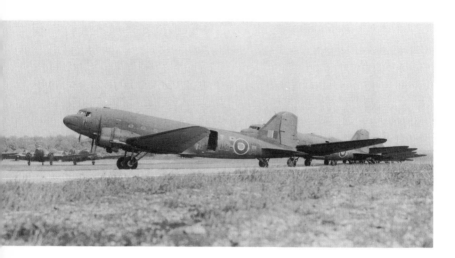

Dakota IIIs of 575 Squadron line up for rapid take off from Broadwell. FZ695:19-A *took part in both Operation* Tonga *and* Mallard *on* D-Day. *(IWM.)*

often from Coulombes (B6). Such activity continued at fever pitch throughout that summer, Dakotas returning with both stretcher cases and walking wounded before mid-September brought the tragedy of Arnhem.

Broadwell's contribution on 17 September comprised 22 aircraft of 512 Squadron and 24 of 575 Squadron with one from 437 Squadron, each Dakota towing a Horsa glider. Low cloud base during take off led to five glider pilots casting off before the Suffolk coast was reached. The pilot of another glider was

In the weeks after D-Day Dakotas were soon flying vital supply missions to France and back to Broadwell.

killed by machine-gun fire near Ousta-houet. Finally, 41 gliders carrying 544 troops of the 1st Border Regiment No 1 Airborne Division along with 22 jeeps, 13 trailers, thirty motor cycles, seventeen ordinary cycles, 34 hand carts and seven anti-tank guns, were launched onto a landing zone west of Arnhem. All Broad-well's Dakotas returned safely.

Resupply on 18 September involved 24 Broadwell Dakotas. One crew cap-tained by Flying Officer Henry flew in error on to a southerly route towards the LZ and Henry was killed when AA guns opened up south of Turnhout. His naviga-tor was wounded and the aircraft's rudder badly damaged before the second pilot took over. The initial inten-tion was to turn back and release the glider over British lines. Instead, its pilots at once cast off, giving Warrant Officer Smith and the Dakota an easier chance of reaching home. He landed safely at Martlesham. A Dakota of 575 Squadron was involved in an alarming incident over the DZ when the tow rope from an aircraft overhead wound itself around the wing of Flying Officer McTeare's machine mak-ing it very difficult to fly, before he landed at Framlingham. One Dakota of 512 Squadron did not return.

On 19 September, thirty Dakotas oper-ated, both Broadwell squadrons each losing an aircraft. Next day 31 crews were involved and 512 Squadron lost another Dakota. With the situation at Arnhem desperate it was decided to place one Dakota squadron much nearer to the dropping zones. On 23 Sep-tember crews of sixteen Dakotas of 512 Squadron found themselves taking per-sonnel of 575 Squadron to B56 (Brus-sels/Evere) with that squadron's eighteen Dakotas tagging along. Late in the afternoon 575 Squadron set out to drop food and ammunition west of Graves. About 75 per cent of the supplies appeared to reach Allied troops, so a second operation was ordered. Eventu-ally four aircraft took off next day and faced plentiful flak.

On 25 September, seven crews oper-ated to a dropping zone west of Arnhem where nearly 800 men were desperate

for supplies. This time the formation flew to Antwerp to meet its fighter escort before unloading 79 panniers of rations, 28 of medical supplies and three bundles of bedding. There was again much machine-gun fire which damaged four Dakotas. All returned except KG 449 which was hit on the port elevator and rudder, but which flew on quite well. Some ten miles north-west of Eindhoven the aircraft then ran into intense flak which put the port engine out of use. Nevertheless it flew on whilst gradually losing height and force landed near Pael, the crew having a lucky escape.

Arnhem passed, the round was again transportation of various loads to the Continent and returning with casualties. For Operation Varsity Broadwell's Dako-tas advanced to Gosfield. After the drop they landed at B56, returning to Broad-well on 25 March. No reduction in the number of sorties flown followed the end of hostilities in Europe, for troops needed supplies and there was repatriation flying to be done. The immediate post-war phase ended for 512 and 575 Squadrons when they moved to Melbourne and Holme-on-Spalding Moor on 6 August 1945. Replacing them were 10 and 76 Squadrons, here to equip with Dakotas prior to Far East service. On 29 August 1945, 77 and 78 Squadrons began to arrive for similar conversion. Soon the move of 78 Squadron was halted; it was instead to go to the Middle East.

Conversion of these squadrons was rapid, 10 and 76 having set off for St Mawgan and Portreath on 28 August. Training was intense at Broadwell, the two squadrons completing 720 glider tows and dropping 2,050 containers. No 77 Squadron left for India in October 1945.

On 5 October 1945, Dakotas of 271 Squadron moved in from Odiham, contin-uing scheduled services within Transport Command's extensive continental net-work. To ease administration Broadwell was switched from 46 to 47 Group on 9 October 1945 and, by December, 271 Squadron was flying on the busy trunk route to India. A 271 Squadron Dakota normally took four days to reach India.

The basic layout of Broadwell captured by a camera in a PR Canberra of 58 Squadron on 31 May 1957. Domestic sites are to the left of the airfield whose runways and 'spectacle' dispersal bays can be easily seen. At the top of the picture is shown part of Brize Norton's extended runway.

Broadwell returned to 46 Group early in April 1946. Throughout that year 271 Squadron concentrated on passenger and freight services mainly to Europe and areas where British Forces were stationed.

Closure of Broadwell was discussed towards the end of 1946, likewise a new siting of 271 Squadron. At the end of October 1946, Bicester was announced as chosen, but Broadwell had more to offer by way of accommodation — and it had concrete runways. Therefore the move was cancelled. On 1 December 1946, 271 Squadron was renumbered 77 Squadron and it continued the pattern of passenger and freight services to, among others, Warsaw, Rome, Prague and particularly Buckeburg. Broadwell's end was not far off and 17 December 1946 most of 77 Squadron left for Manston. With the rear party of 77 Squadron gone by 9 January 1947, closure began and 31 March 1947 marked the last day of RAF tenure of Broadwell.

Chalgrove

SU635980. 10 miles SE of Oxford by the B480
Following an early breakfast on 20 November 1943 a few RAF men left HQ 70 Group, Farnborough, to undertake a mighty mission. Travelling in 3 ton trucks, 30 cwt vans and two lighter ones — and superintended by the party's commanding officer in a car — they arrived at Chalgrove, a muddy mess.

Its readiness was nil. Not even a telephone had been installed to allow the news to reach a wider audience. Within a day a consignment of bicycles came from Andover. Many had flat tyres and the absence of even one pump rendered them decidedly 'U/S'. As the occupants viewed their plight, a great consignment of 'iron bedsteads' landed, complete with a vast number of 'biscuits'. Four days after opening time a GPO man came to enquire whether Chalgrove's occupants might need a telephone. A request was filed to HQ 70 Group for something akin, and for two battery radios for a station totally divorced from everything, including the world situation in which it might have to play a part.

On 26 November 1943 a telephone arrived — for viewing only. In desperation, and perhaps fearing the worst, an officer completed an overland pilgrimage to Benson in an attempt to contact their padre. Surely he could enlist help for all? Indeed, his power was sufficient, and comfort came — in the form of Woodbines and rare bars of chocolate.

By Sunday equipment was submerging all and sundry. From distant Peterhead on 30 November came a new commanding officer, Squadron Leader H. A. Mockton, MM. That event interested a passing Miles Magister the following morning. To encourage the inmates of 'Chalgrove-in-the-Mud' it decided to pay a call, producing a milestone in the station's history. Evidently neither it nor its crew liked what they saw for the 'Maggie' swung round and promptly left in the opposite direction to which it had landed. It was foggy so a hasty call to Benson was made. Thank goodness that telephone was now working! The folks there fired, doubtless with great glee, a signal mortar bomb.

To the surprise of all, the Maggie's pre-emptive opening of Chalgrove raised it to international airport standard for, later that day, a Lockheed P-38 Lightning landed — and stayed. True, that stay was brief. The pilot appeared to take one glance at Chalgrove before hastily departing. He had apparently arrived where he did not want to be. Another early arrival, an Oxford which touched down on 3 December, brought in a pilot who, upon enquiring where he was and being told 'Chalgrove', looked blank and said he couldn't 'find the place' on his map. He, too, fled to the comfort of Benson and, it later transpired, left to follow the railway lines towards London in order to reach Heston. Later it was discovered that the occupants were Americans who presumably had hijacked this RAF-marked Oxford!

The most significant event since the RAF moved in came with the arrival of Colonel F. M. Paul, US Air Service Command, bringing plans for a 9th US Air

Force invasion of the station. Far more important though was the proximity of Christmas. Traditionally officers wait upon other ranks during the Christmas dinner but at Chalgrove far greater things were to overcome all. Turkey and trimmings duly scoffed, pudding — then the impossible. In Britain, wracked by war shortages, each man on camp was astonished to be awarded a real, round, juicy orange. So rare was it that many in wartime Britain had never sighted one. So unusual were these bright objects that few were eaten. The suggestion was that Chalgrove's precious supply be taken home, shown to the children and maybe closetted in glass cases and labelled *Orangus Americanus* or something similar.

The 'locals' also had taken pity on the 'mud-men' and upon this special day, braved up to inviting seventeen of them into their homes to share what joy there was — and, maybe, gaze with awe and pre-war dreams upon an orange. Not so Mrs Preston, good soul, who gave up her day of happiness to help with the washing-up at the camp and then mend some woollens.

At the end of December a giant American airplane, a C-47, touched down with a load of Americans coming to capture this rebel outpost. Captain Hay announced that many more Americans were about to march off a big ship to revitalize this tatty British stronghold and make it great. With the announcement that 2,000 were coming, and 'many officers', there was general panic. Maybe that explains why, at this late hour in the war against Germany, although there were few enemy aircraft about 'shelters' were dug. But, as quickly as he came, Captain May disappeared. Perhaps Chalgrove would still be a nice, quiet place when the spring came? Alas no, for 6 January brought proof of what was pending, with the arrival of a Lieutenant Colonel E. Haight to command the 9th AF Americans.

Three days later they came out of the mist ... 400, at the unwelcome hour of 05:10. They seemed to delight in moving in great convoys, unable to resist the allure of night life except for military operations! I used to think they did it to bring fun and surprise to us all. Another curious habit they displayed was delight in leaning out of lorry cabs, as foreigners lean out of trains. It made the passage of American vehicles extremely hazardous for hapless cyclists who, whether they liked it or not, frequently became recipients of chewed (or unchewed) 'gum'.

Nature greeted the arrival by the occupying power at Chalgrove with torrential rain. These Americans had come from Culham railway station, and welcoming them to Oxfordshire was the task of Chalgrove's Adjutant who had been compelled to arise at 03:00. He later referred to his role as 'sacrificial to Anglo-US relations'. He was rewarded, though for he soon proclaimed himself drunk on real, US Official coffee. Nevertheless, he brightened sufficiently to be fully awake as the troop train pulled in. His ordeal, was far from over for he had not been able to acquire an Anglo-US phrase book. There was much to conquer.

By mid-January 1944 about 1,000 Americans had penetrated Chalgrove. Some of the original RAF party had escaped to Kingston Bagpuize only to face the terror all over again! Then, at the turn of the month, there came the business end of the new world, the arrival of 45 officers and 297 men of Chalgrove's first operational unit, the 30th PR Squadron USAAF.

Whilst the new unit sorted itself out, Chalgrove had most unlikely intruders, two intrepid Englishmen announcing themselves as Sub Lieutenant Fellows, an FAA pilot, and Mr P. Goodsir, from Thame, here to enquire whether they might borrow the airfield for the testing of model gliders built by International Model Aircraft, known universally to pre-war aviation enthusiasts as those people who produced the lovely 'Frog Penguins'. Goodsir was the glider's designer and runways were needed for the tests. These Thame did not have. Squadron Leader Monckton agreed and on 10 February 1944 two gliders arrived by road. One was quickly erected and next morning a Defiant and a Martinet came to

A Royal Navy Vengeance TT IV waits at Chalgrove to tow away a Lines Brothers' target glider.

undertake some towing.

When all was ready, 'little America' paused as Chalgrove's first International air display was about to take place. After a lot of checking a combination began to roll. Towing off needed some pluck for it was hard enough to tow away a manned glider, let alone this pilotless one. Satisfied with his preliminary checks, Flight Sergeant R. Hitchin chanced his luck and the Martinet and glider flew well away, to the delight of the audience. Landing with the target glider in tow successfully accomplished, another glider, with twice the wing span of the first, was attached to the tow rope and flew just as successfully. A feasible proposition became a certainty. International Models produced the target gliders which saw wartime and post-war service.

Already Chalgrove's first operational aircraft had arrived, P-38 Lightnings. One engaged a Spitfire in mock combat in which the lighter, British fighter totally out-performed its friend. That happened on St Valentine's Day 1944; the final stage in the marriage of the two air forces took place the next day.

The band of the US 9th AF, at the usual pace of such organizations, hurried on to the tarmac which, at a wartime airfield, was the nearest thing to a parade ground. Behind trailed the brave British warriors keeping company with Benson's Colour Party. As the national anthem sounded the RAF Ensign was lowered in colonial, ceremonial style. To suppressed satisfaction, in its place was raised a very tattered Stars and Stripes, a ceremony requiring the might of five Uncle Sams. As the Old Glory fluttered a bit, the strains of 'The Star Spangled Banner' wafted across Chalgrove's wastes, now drying out a little — and all the guards showed their arms. Chalgrove was USAAF Station No 465. The 'Yanks' had come, and a tale was ended that had been repeated many times elsewhere.

Their purpose in coming was virtually singlefold. They were here to invade and

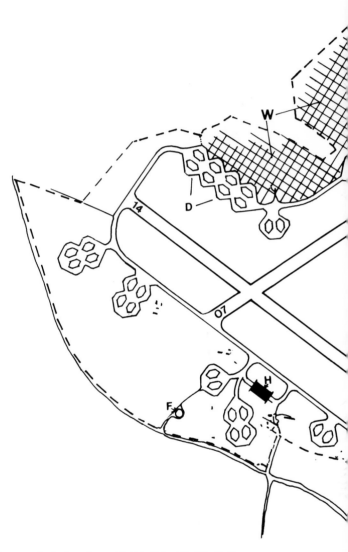

Chalgrove, a typical wartime airfield built for US IXth Air Force use. **C** Control tower **D** 50 Loop type hard standings **F** Fuel dump (75,000 gallons) **H** Two Type T2 hangars **L** Domestic sites **P** Photographic block **T** Technical site **W** Weapons storage area. Runway 14/32 2,000 yd, 25/07 and 19/01 each 1,400 yd.

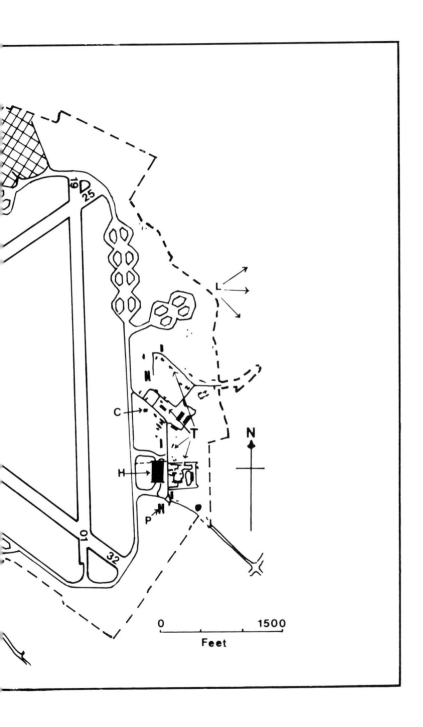

0   1500

Feet

repossess France — with some outside help. All training would be fast, furious and directed to that singular purpose. Chalgrove would be the base from which photographic and visual reconnaissance of enemy forces in France would take place prior to, and following, the Normandy landings. It would provide information for attack squadrons operating from East Anglia and southern England.

The first to arrive, the 30th Photographic Reconnaisance Squadron, joined the 9th AF on 4 February 1944 to become part of the 10th Photographic Group on 21 February. Standard equipment became varieties of the P-38 for photo-reconnaissance. On 23 March the 31st Photographic Reconnaissance Squadron became established within the 10th, and six days later it was joined by the 34th Squadron. The Group was raised to full strength by the arrival on 27 April of the 33rd Squadron.

Assigned to the Group was a variety of PR tasks, particularly low-level operations. Photographs were secured of enemy airfields and especially coastal defences and ports prior to the Normandy landings. Damage assessment material was gathered following 9th AF attacks on airfields, marshalling yards, bridges and tactical targets. Marauder crews could study the success of their operations. The 10th's low level 232 — sortie photo survey of the coast from Blankenburg to Dunkirk — a strongly defended zone — and from Le Touquet to St Vaast-la-Houge between 6 May and 20 May 1944, won a Distinguished Unit Citation. By June the assortment of aircraft at Chalgrove included F-3s, F-5s, F-6s and light liaison aircraft.

As soon as the Allies landed in France the Group began a fast, furious campaign, photographing enemy troop concentrations, bridges, artillery posts, road and rail junctions, airfields and any enemy targets about which it was necessary to be well informed — and for neutralizing resistance during the breakout from the Normandy beach-head at St Lô. On 27 June 1944 the 15th Tactical Reconnaissance Squadron was transferred from the 67th Tactical Reconnais-sance Group to the 10th and brought its P-51s and F-6s to Chalgrove. They replaced the 30th PR Squadron which, on 9 June 1944, moved to Middle Wallop and the 67th Tactical Reconnaissance Group. With the advance well underway the 10th packed its bags and in mid-August moved rapidly to an airfield near Rennes. Chalgrove's operational span was brief but vital, and it remained in American hands as a base for C-47 Dakotas.

A rearrangement of the USAAFs PR units came in March 1945. It brought the 7th Photographic Group (Reconnaissance) from Mount Farm to Chalgrove in the closing days of the war. On 26 March the 22nd PR Squadron flew its P-51s and F-5s here, and was followed by the 14th Squadron on 2 April, the 13th on 8 April and the 27th which returned from France on 22 April after the Rhine crossing had been accomplished. In the immediate post-war period there was much reconnaissance and photographic work for these squadrons in assessing the plight of Europe from the air and providing damage assessment data for peaceful purposes. That continued until mid-October 1945 when the 7th Group split, with the 13th Squadron moving to Grove on 13 October as the 14th and 22nd Squadrons moved to Villacoublay. The 27th Squadron vacated Chalgrove for Germany on 14 October 1945, but it was December before the Group HQ finally left Chalgrove.

Between 6 August and November 1945 Chalgrove held Mosquito PR XVIs of the 653rd Bomb Squadron which had been taken from the 25th Bomb Group in August 1944 to provide weather reconnaissance flights for the 9th AF. On 21 November 1945 the 7th Reconnaissance Group was de-activated at Chalgrove following the posting of its squadrons overseas.

After the Americans left, the station came under Benson's control. By 1946 agreement was reached for Martin Baker to use Chalgrove. Their factory was near Denham and a suitable airfield was needed for test purposes. On 24 July 1946, when flying in a Meteor at 8,600 ft

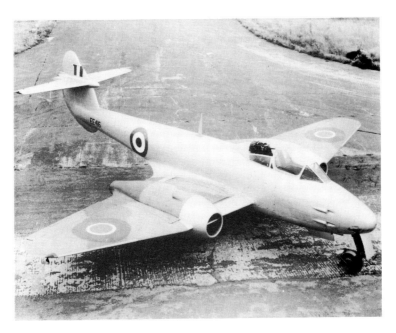

Using Meteor III EE416, Martin-Baker Ltd carried out the first in-flight ejection (of a dummy) on 14 June 1946. Then on 24 July Bernard Lynch of the firm made the first live ejection, again from EE416. (Martin-Baker Ltd.)

and 320 knots over the airfield, Mr Bernard Lynch, a Martin Baker employee and a volunteer, made the first live ejection from a Martin Baker ejector seat. A year later the Mk 1 seat was ordered for fitment in RAF and RN fighters.

Remnants of 8 OTU, which had provided operational training for pilots and observers for the RAFs photo-reconnaissance squadrons, shared Chalgrove with the civilians. The unit arrived on 4 July 1946 and left in October

In 1952 Martin-Baker received the hybrid Meteor WA634, parts of which were from the original T Mk 7 while the rear fuselage and tail unit were from a Mk 8. For ten years WA634 flew from Chalgrove as the ejector seat test vehicle, then in April 1962 it was retired. It currently forms part of the aircraft collection at RAF Cosford. (Martin-Baker Ltd.)

Two ejector seat test bed Meteors, WA638 and WA634, stand at Chalgrove alongside a Hunter T 7. WA638 remains at Chalgrove. (Martin-Baker Ltd.)

1946, taking with it three Spitfire XIs and two Mosquito PR 34s. There was still some flying from here by Benson-based Mosquitoes and Spitfires.

Since the 1940s Chalgrove has been Martin Baker's test airfield and the home of a Meteor, a Dove and, until 1981, the Company's Dakota. The two-seater Meteor permits test ejections to a speed of 450 knots. Around the airfield's perimeter is a high wire fence. There are few buildings, but a 'T2' hangar remains along with, naturally, well-maintained perimeter track and runway.

Caught in the act! A recent test ejection from yet another Meteor hybrid, WL419, which has been used since 1979. (Martin-Baker Ltd.)

Chipping Norton

SP325255. 2 miles S of Chipping Norton, by B4026

Few who travel to the Cotswolds fail to discover Chipping Norton whose name derives from the medieval word, Chepynge, which describes the long, narrow market place. Of the airfield, an enhanced RLG, more remains than might be expected — there are concrete huts and air raid shelters by the road, and an unexpected survivor in good condition is the rifle range.

First to use the landing ground was 15 SFTS. Upon being pushed out of Middle Wallop by 10 Group, Oxfords of the Advanced Training Squadron came to Chipping Norton where Headquarters 15 SFTS arrived on 10 July 1940.

The airfield stood on a confined area 70 ft above sea level. Three grass runways were marked out in July 1940, the NW/SE of 1,000 yds, the E/W of 800 yds and N/S of 600 yds. The overshoot was disturbing, for the land dropped away to the south-west. In 1940 two Bellman hangars and a few wooden huts comprised the technical site. Personnel were billetted in Bell tents neatly lined in one corner. Stores and messing arrangements were by the B4026 road, and main water was drawn from a temporary link to Chipping Norton's supply. All electricity was generated at the camp. During July 1940, 15 SFTS started to equip with Harvard Is, twenty being at the RLG by the end of the month. There were also 27 Oxfords here and remains of R6266 which had crashed into a stationary Oxford *(N4580)* causing both to be burnt. Three days later Oxford *P1890* collided with *N6326* over Charlebury with shattering results. At this time HQ 15 SFTS was in Oldner House, Chipping Norton — about one mile north of the airfield.

On 2 August 1940 the unit was informed that it was to be consolidated at Kidlington, but the Advanced Training Squadron remained some time at Chipping Norton. On 31 August 1940 the squadron's return showed 41 Harvards and 15 Oxfords as based here. Headquarters staff moved to Kidlington on 1 October 1940, the remainder going on 13 October when the aerodrome came into use as Kidlington's RLG. The enemy called on 29-30 October — and their brand of nightlites were distributed nearby. Some high-explosive bombs

Long-time survivor, the rifle range at Chipping Norton in 1981.

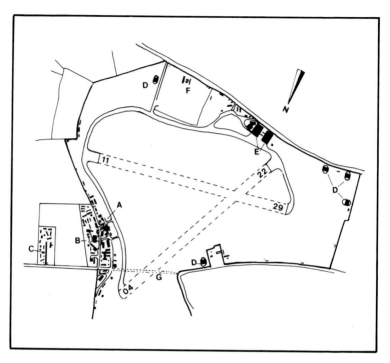

*Chipping Norton in 1943 shows the features of a satellite training station with limited development. The technical site **A** lies to the south of the road through the camp, the instruction site **B** to the north. **C** marks sub-site 5 (a domestic area) and Blister hangars (Extra Over Type 69 ft) are marked **D**. That in the most southerly corner was Over Type 65 ft. Two Bellman Hangars are marked **E**. Remaining in quite good condition are the machine gun butts (147/41). An interesting feature was the dummy road crossing Runway 04/22 (marked **G**).*

were dropped a mile to the east on 5-6 November.

At the end of 1940, Kidlington's RLGs were reconsidered, changes becoming effective in February 1941, releasing this RLG from 15 SFTS control. Since 16 November 1940 it had been in the hands of 6 SFTS, Little Rissington which positioned Oxfords here, particularly for night flying. The Luftwaffe welcomed 6 SFTS by placing several HEs on the landing ground on 18-19 November 1940;.

Extended facilities constructed in 1941-42 included a watch office (13726/41) and an instruction site to the rear of the technical area. Four Over Type 69 ft Blister hangars and a single

Over Type 65 ft supplemented the Bellman hangars, and two Sommerfeld runways were laid on QDMs 11/29 and 04/22. Unusually, the perimeter track only partially circled the field. Sub Site 1 held the engine repair facilities, general maintenance, servicing and stores buildings. On Site 2 were placed the ground staff room and flight offices. Dormitory huts (2965/42) and ablutions were found at Site 5.

From November 1940 Chipping Norton was under 6 SFTS control, that unit becoming 6 (P) AFU on 1 April 1942. To the end of the war it was used by their Oxfords remaining with 6 (P) AFU until it closed on December 1945. The site was disposed of in the 1950s.

Cowley

SP555035, 3 miles SE of Oxford, along the A4142

Varied were the Civilian Repair depots, factories giant or small to which damaged aircraft were taken for repair, cannibalization or complete write-off. Largest was No 1 Civilian Repair Unit, Cowley, which handled Hurricanes and Spitfires. Officially opened on 11 September 1939, Cowley CRU was functioning by the outbreak of war, crews of No 50 MU recovering aircraft to be worked upon. From early 1940, No 1 Metal Produce and Recovery Depot assisted. All were mainly civilian manned and headed by Lord Nuffield.

Part of his Morris factory was converted into aircraft workshops. Flight test hangars were provided and a grass landing ground alongside had two runways. This superceded the use of Abingdon for flight testing in Spring 1940. No 1 CRU provided vital back-up during the Battle of Britain, its civilian staff working night and day to return damaged aircraft to MUs and squadrons. Although Spitfires remained the principal wartime commodity — because of Nuffield's intended association with them through Castle Bromwich — many other aircraft types were repaired here until hostilities ceased. Then the reversion of factory and airfield to civilian state was rapid. Some buildings used by 1 CRU remain, but the airfield has long since gone and partly rests beneath the Oxford Ring Road.

Wrecked aircraft unsuitable for repair went to Cowley in vast quantities from mid-1940. From them was extracted mainly alloy, but also rubber and plastic. Giant heaps of barely recognizable items accumulated and salvage continued long after the war. By then No 1 MPRD was handling huge numbers of aircraft scrapped after hostilities, some without even a solitary day of military service. Close proximity of Nos 6 and 8 MUs led to many aircraft being dismembered here.

Cowley factory played another part in the war effort — the production of over 3,000 Tiger Moths. Argument has long raged over the precise number constructed, for there were many spares items made. Certainly Cowley's wartime Tiger Moth production was considerable, and many a 'Tiger' still flying originated at the Morris works.

Culham

SU052958, 1½ miles SE of Abingdon, by A415

On dry land close to Oxford once rested HMS *Hornbill*, an unexpected sight where now stands Culham Laboratory, an expansive nuclear establishment. Hangars of the former occupant may be seen on its north-west side. *Hornbill* was commissioned on 1 November 1944 as an Aircraft Receipt and Despatch Unit. It attracted many types of aircraft for the RN Ferry Pool (later known as No 1 Ferry Flight) was based here, using Ansons, Fireflies, Reliants and Seafires.

Culham's principal use was as a centre for naval reservists residing between London and Oxford and the surrounds. To train them 1832 Squadron was commissioned on 1 July 1947 and used Seafire IIIs, XVs, XVIIs and FR 46s. Harvard IIbs and Mk IIIs also served the squadron and Sea Fury FB 11s later. A move to Benson came on 18 July 1953 as part of Culham's run down. No 1840 RNVR Squadron formed here from 1832 Squadron on 14 April 1951, and operated Firefly Is, IVs and Harvards before leaving for Ford on 30 June 1951.

Two further reserve squadrons commissioned on 1 October 1952 were Nos 1832A and 1832B which became 1836 and 1835 Squadrons respectively in April 1953, prior to moving to the Southern Air Division Benson on 18 July 1953 and taking their Sea Fury FB 11s.

An interesting small unit which formed here on 11 May 1947 was 739 Squadron, known also as the Photographic Trials and Development Unit, equipped with Sea Mosquito TR 33s, Sea Hornet F 20s and PR 22s and a Dominie. Culham's aircraft carried the tail identity letters 'CH'.

Above *About to touch down on Culham's main runway, Seafire F XVII 106/CH.* (FAA Museum.)

Above left *Seafire line-up at Culham with an F Mk XV SW910:123/CH nearest and three Mk XVIIs beyond.* (FAA Museum.)

Left *Two Mk XVII Seafires at Culham, SP343:126/CH and SX198:101/CH. In the distance lurk Sea Vampires.* (FAA Museum.)

Right *An aerial view of RNAS Culham.* (FAA Museum.)

CONCRETE RUNWAYS.
ALL WEATHER
SURFACE
LEFT HAND CIRCUIT

RN AIR STATION
CULHAM
51 39N I 13W
HEIGHT 200FT ASL

R/T FACILITIES
H/F AND VH/F LOCAL CONTROL
ONLY
HOMING FACILITIES
V.G BEACON OROO-I6OO
251W ON REQUEST NO D/F

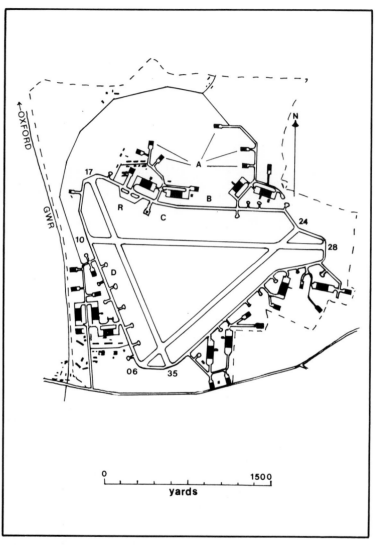

Culham was completed in the autumn of 1944 as a Receipt and Despatch Unit for the Royal Navy. It had three tarmac runways, 06/24 (1,200 yd × 30 yd), (1,400 yd × 30 yd) and 17/35 (1,200 yd × 30 yd). An unusual feature was the distribution of hangars **A** around the entire perimeter track. Of these, 21 (one for squadron use, twenty as storage hangars) measured 87 ft 6 in by 60 ft and had a door height of 17 ft and width of 55 ft. A further eleven hangars **B**, one of which was used for modifying and erecting aircraft, measured 185 ft by 105 ft. Their main use was for aircraft servicing. **C** marks the position of the control tower and **R** the refuelling apron. The main domestic site was to the north-east of the landing ground.

HMS *Hornbill* paid off on 30 September 1953, subsequent to which the Admiralty used Culham as a store until the Atomic Energy Commission moved in during early 1960.

Edgehill

SP365435. 9 miles WNW of Banbury, near Shenington, off the A422
Edgehill was completed in October 1941 as a satellite for 21 OTU, Moreton-in-the-Marsh. Although opened on 21 October 1941, flights from here by ageing Wellington 1cs had begun in August. It seems that 12 OTU also made early use of the station.

On 14 May 1941, the Gloster E28/39 Pioneer *W4041* first flew at Cranwell and, after ten hours flying, returned by road to Gloucester for a new engine. Returning the Pioneer to Cranwell had disadvantages, that airfield being far from Glos-

*Edgehill began as a rudimentary landing ground, then was much improved into becoming a bomber airfield satellite station. Take-off towards the west meant passage over the steep scarp face, for which reason the control tower **A** had additional height for a watch to be kept.*

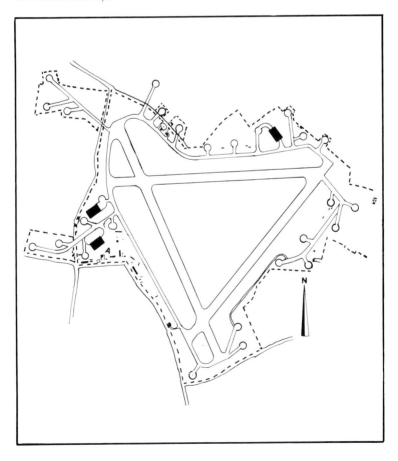

ter's home. Closer sites to Brockworth were examined, also alternatives in reasonable reach of the Power Jets' centre at Lutterworth. Eventually, Edgehill was selected. Brockworth was too small and too close to hilly ground, for which reason Stoke Orchard was also unsuitable.

Edgehill with one 1,600 yd and two 1,200 yd runways was, rather like Barford, situated on a plateau. Its position, though, was unusual because at the western end the ground fell away in a dramatic scarp face to a valley below. Nevertheless the approaches to the airfield were unobstructed so, despite that fall-away, it was reckoned suitable for the task, a special Robin hangar being erected to house the jet in secrecy. The agreement was for the Pioneer to fly from Edgehill and the F9/40 fighter from Cranwell or Newmarket during 1942.

To Edgehill W4041 came, powered by a W.1A engine. It made its first trial taxi on 4 February 1942. Flight testing began and, with this new engine, the Pioneer was quieter in flight and flew smoothly until trouble struck on 24 March 1942. Part of a turbine blade broke away in flight and the aircraft hurriedly landed at Edgehill.

Wellington 1cs and Ansons of 21 OTU were very active at this time and used the airfield for training purposes. From here 21 OTU despatched a dozen Wellington 1cs for the Cologne raid of May 30-31 1942 and DV598, taking off, hit a tree. Two other crews aborted leaving nine to complete their sorties. In the Essen raid eleven crews operated, and ten took part in the June 1,000 Plan Bremen attack when X3179 failed to return.

Flight trials of W4041 were resumed by 'Jerry' Sayer in June 1942, but not without moments of concern. Fuel starvation was encountered and a flame-out also

Mock hedgerows can be seen to have been painted across Edgehill's almost completely disguised landing ground and runways, in this photograph taken on 6 October 1942. (RAF Museum.)

brought a quick return, among the Wellingtons, to Edgehill. Throughout that hot summer the jet was test flown and on 27 September 1942 a group of visitors arrived for a demonstration, among them Americans. Just as the Pioneer was getting airborne the oil pressure fell very low and, conserving what he had while reducing power, Sayer was seen to sink below the edge of the escarpment. Great relief greeted his safe pulling away. He kept his speed low and made a neat, forced landing. Not many days later whilst flying a Typhoon off the north-east coast, Sayer was killed, possibly in collision with another aircraft. His place was taken by Michael Daunt, although it was November 1942 before he began flying the E28/39. After four flights, W4041 was conveyed by lorry to Farnborough for engine development work, whilst 21 OTU's Wellingtons continued to drone around the circuit. Flying was interrupted at this time by some runway resurfacing.

Since 1940, Power Jets Ltd, who built Whittle's engines, had been linked with Rover, which was to build production versions of the Whittle W.2 engine. MAP placed a contract on 4 August 1940 for such work to proceed at Coventry. For greater safety it was soon switched to the Clitheroe works in Lancashire. Rover began in 1942 the design of their jet engine, the B.26, which started running trials in November 1942. At this time Rolls-Royce took over Rover's work on gas turbines.

In February 1943 the second Gloster E28/39, W4046, powered by a Rover W.2B engine, was taken to Edgehill. It first flew during the evening of 1 March 1943, the pilot being John Grierson. During early flight trials it reached just over 400 mph after an unstick run of 330 yards. Such success was sufficient to permit it to be flown to Hatfield on 17 April 1943 for a few days of demonstration flying, that 19½ minute flight being the first cross country journey undertaken, although it

The remains of Edgehill's control tower.

was nowhere near as ambitious as that of the F9/40's first such venture. Very strict flying limits were laid down for the early jets, and from Edgehill they were only allowed to venture up to five miles away or fly within a corridor two miles wide between Edgehill and Cheltenham, a distance of about 30 miles. The duration of early jet aircraft was very limited. On 3 May 1943, *W4046* was taken to RAE Farnborough and Gloster's use of it ceased. This brought an end to jet flying at Edgehill.

That event came about shortly after another period of upheaval for, on 12 April 1943, No 12 OTU, based at Chipping Warden, took over the station from 21 OTU. Two Flights of the Unit under Wing Commander C. W. Scott arrived from Turweston on 27 April 1943 and used Wellington IIIs. These began to be replaced by Wellington Xs in August 1943. Edgehill was used to accommodate 12 OTU's gunnery flight's Martinets and Hurricanes as well as the initial training element of the OTU, until the unit closed early June 1945.

Visit the site now and a few typical wartime airfield buildings can still be seen. Most unusual is the wartime control tower which has one storey more than usual, presumably to afford a better view of aircraft as they sped over that scarp face.

Enstone

SP395255. 5½ miles SE of Chipping Norton, by B4030
Although Enstone opened as a second satellite for 21 OTU, Moreton-in-the-Marsh on 15 September 1942 it did not come into use until 12 April 1943, replacing Edgehill. Wellington 1cs remained here until April 1944, Mk IIIs having been phased in late in 1943 and Wellington Xs, February–March 1944. No 21 OTU's X Flight (Gunnery) arrived on 17 May 1943 equipped with Martinets, and left for Moreton-in-the-Marsh on 24 February 1944.

From Enstone, 21 OTU carried out leaflet dropping operations over France, an unusual activity from a satellite. Inter-esting arrivals from Stanton Harcourt, on 26 February 1944, were five Curtiss Tomahawks of No 1682 Bomber Defence Training Flight, which used Enstone until disbandment on 21 August 1944. From April 1944 the Flight was Hurricane equipped, Tomahawks leaving in May.

No 21 OTU had a post-war existence, although the unit used Honeybourne from August to October 1945. Flying ceased at Enstone in November 1945 and Enstone passed to Maintenance Command on 17 January 1946. On 28 October 1946 it was placed under the control of Flying Training Command, and a detachment of Oxfords and Harvards of 17 SFTS, Coleby Grange, arrived on 10 November and stayed until 17 December 1946 when they moved to Moreton-in-the-Marsh to form the basis of No 1 Refresher School. Enstone subsequently saw limited use as Little Rissington's RLG.

Although the RAF left long ago, flying has not ceased here. An active gliding club, the Enstone Eagles, uses the control tower and a good runway, at one time used for surface trials. Microlights and light aircraft also use the aerodrome. Whereas at many airfields contractors smash concrete, at Enstone they busily make it, at an industrial area embracing the hangar and wartime buildings at the east end of the airfield.

Finmere

SP250300. 5 miles W of Buckingham, by A421
Finmere had a very curious layout. Runway 06/25 was parallel to the A421 Oxford road, its intersection with the other two runways at the northern tip of the former. From the air Finmere appeared to have runways radiating from a hub near the juction of the A421 and B4031 roads. Since the closure of the airfield for military purposes, the Preston Bisset road has been placed across taxi tracks leading from the east/west runway. Finmere was one of the few airfields with a watch office placed almost in the middle of the landing ground; unusual

too, was its siting close to a runway. Adjacent to the tower were the flight and aircrew offices. Bomb dumps were to be found to the north-west of where the remaining good state 'B1' hangar (pattern 11776/42) is still to be seen. There was only one other hangar at Finmere, a 'T2' (8259/40) now used by Midland Shires Farmers.

Indicative of the station's importance, particularly late in the war, was the number of huts for personnel. Officers and sergeants had living quarters in either Laing or Nissen huts. Airmen were billeted in Nissen huts (9024/41). Ablutions were in temporary brick buildings.

A landing ground at Finmere was used by Blenheims of 13 OTU Bicester early in 1941, but it was 1942 before it was really established as an airfield. Form the start of August 1942, the station came fully under the control of Bicester as a satellite for 13 OTU, and was used by Blenheims, both Mk I and IV. Crews trained for 2 Group and for service overseas, although Blenheims were slowly being supplanted. To supply the Blenheim V squadrons in north-west Africa at the start of 1943, No 307 Ferry Training Unit formed at Bicester on 24 December 1942 and soon after received seven Blenheim Vs. For a week in February 1943 these flew from Finmere because of Bicester's bad state. They briefly kept company with Whitleys of 1473 Flight from Upper Heyford, at Finmere from January 1943 to September 1943. The Flight also used Wellingtons.

A foretaste of Finmere's present style was provided by 1473 Flight's communications aircraft, de Havilland Leopard Moth *AX858* (formerly *G-ACGS*). Early in March 1943, 307 FTU was notified that it was to re-arm with Boston IIIs and train crews to fly them to North Africa, the Blenheim V commitment being soon to end. The FTU moved completely to Finmere on 18 March 1943 to make use of runways there. To assist in crew conversion three Havocs and a couple of Bostons were placed on 307 FTUs permanent strength. The first Boston III, *AL697*, arrived here on 20 March 1943. Another, *Z2197*, was collected from West Raynham on 16 April 1943 and made a trial delivery flight to Gibraltar, taking off from Portreath. The journey time was 6 hours 50 minutes.

Finmere was still in demand for Blenheim training. Relief came when 307 FTU was briefly sited at Turweston, from 1 May 1943 to 18 May. That unit returned as the equipment at Finmere was updated by the arrival of 13 OTUs Mitchell IIs and Boston IIIas. 307 FTU, under 70 Group of Fighter Command, busied itself ferrying Boston to North Africa, despatching its first Bostons on 11 June 1943. During September 1943, 307 FTU started to receive Boston IIIas. On arrival at the FTU, crews trained on the type they would fly, before being allocated the machine which they were to ferry overseas. October 1943 saw the completion of this task and between 9 and 27 October the FTU moved to Melton Mowbray. At the start of November, control of 13 OTU passed to 9 Group. Boston and Mitchell training went ahead at some pace for the next few months.

Early 1944 witnessed a major change for in January 13 OTU began to receive, at Finmere, its first Mosquitoes. Crew training commenced on 14 February, and within the next four weeks 13 OTU's remaining Blenheims were withdrawn. Finmere was now the OTU for 2 Group's Mosquito, Mitchell and Boston crews, the former gradually acquiring the leading part. In the middle of 1944, 13 OTU had 34 Mosquitoes here, and a few Bostons.

When 38 Group vacated Harwell in October 1944 that station was taken over by 13 OTU whose Mosquitoes moved there. This left Boston IVs and Mitchells at Finmere, but not for long because the Mosquito element of 60 OTU (concentrating upon training crews for Mosquito intruder squadrons) arrived during the first two weeks of March 1945. Its Mosquitoes were stationed here, its other aircraft at Hampstead Norris. On 3 March, 2 Group took control of the unit which dissolved into 13 OTU. Boston flying ceased at Finmere on 19 March 1945.

Ironically, training was switched to providing up to eighteen crews monthly

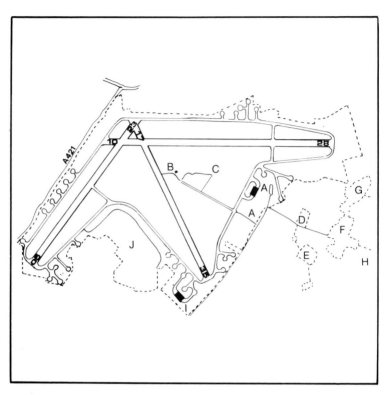

*Finmere can be seen to have a most unusual layout, with runways radiating from the northern tip of the landing ground. **A** marks the technical area, **B** the control tower (13726/41 and modified items), **C** the crew rooms, **D** the instructional site, **E** the WAAF site, **F** the communal site, **G** No 2 accommodation site and **H** No 1 site. Area **J** marks the weapons store, **I** nearby being the B1 hangar still in good condition. The layout as shown approximates to that in the last two years of the war.*

for Mosquito squadrons — not in 2 Group, but in the Far East. At Finmere on 30 April 1945 there were 47 Mosquitoes, mainly Mk IIs, in addition to eight Ansons, a Proctor, Dominie and Tiger Moth within the Mosquito Wing of the new 13 OTU. Orders were received in May for the provision of 31 Mosquito crews monthly. On 28 May 1945 Mitchell training ceased and Finmere soon held the full active strength of the OTU. During June that came to include six of the then very new Tempest IIs. Contraction of the home-based air forces was already under way and in late July 1945, 13 OTU left for

Middleton St George taking 44 Mosquitoes, six Ansons, five Mitchells and the Tempests. Just imagine the trade that one of the frequent Sunday markets or Vintage Aeroplane Club displays at Finmere would generate if a few of those types had been left behind!

Grove

SU395900. W of village, 1 mile N of Wantage
Grove originated in a decision to build a well-equipped three-runway spare bomber airfield for 91 Group. When in

1942 Brize Norton became a glider pilot training centre instead of a bomber OTU, Grove logically slipped under that station's control. In August 1942, Wellingtons of 15 OTU had made use of the airfield for Grove was intended to replace Hampstead Norris as Harwell's satellite at the time. With so much gliding activity close by, it was inadvisable for that scheme to go forward and Grove was transferred to Flying Training Command.

Over the first four months of 1943, Brize Norton's Whitleys and Horsas used the airfield, and on 11-12 March 1943 Typhoons of 174 and 184 Squadrons were here taking part in Exercise *Spartan*. Well into 1943 the airfield remained far from complete, and it seems likely that Grove had already been earmarked for American use. Different use of the station came in early May 1943 when Oxfords of K, L and M Flights of 15 (P)AFU were brought here and also temporarily used Greenham Common and Ramsbury. All were earmarked to become US 9th AF transport bases. When 15 (P)AFU arrived the runways remained incomplete, and the airfield surface left much to be desired, being amply marred by depressions and ditches. Ever increased flying made the area heavily congested too, so 15 (P)AFU moved to Andover in July 1943 and its Oxfords vacated Grove on 3 July 1943.

The US 9th AAF Support Command took control and used Grove as a repair and maintenance base for C-47 Dakotas and later for C-46 Commandos. Communications flights of the 9th AAF were here in 1944, using Proctors, Oxfords, UC-64s and UC-78s.

A dramatic event took place on 2 March 1944 when the exotic Vickers Armstrongs Windsor *DW506* force-landed here and was written off as a result. The accident occurred in poor weather when the large, unconventional and highly secret bomber was being flown by a pilot new to the type. A piece of metal had become lodged in the constant speed unit of the starboard inner propeller, as a result of which the engine could not be feathered. In the crash the bomber broke its back.

By the end of the war Grove had an unconventional appearance. Among the assortment of buildings of 1941, 1942 and 1943 vintage were six 'T2' hangars (3653/42) one being purely set aside for use as a store for aircraft parts. Two others were used as assembly shops, while in two Robin hangars (2204/41) parts salvaged from crashed aircraft, and also propellers, were held. The airfield had 78 dispersal standings, mainly on the east side. On the west was the bomb store, a reminder of the original plan.

In February 1946 the RAF took over the station, its excellent facilities being used both as an RLG and by 6 MU Brize Norton, the busily disposing of wartime surplus aircraft. It later became No 431 Equipment Depot, 2nd TAF probably being reopened after care and maintenance about 1954. Runways had been resurfaced and flying control reopened, but the station was unable to support the projected transport operations whereby the station would be a depot for equipment needed in Germany. Training flights were made by Balliols based at Benson, but little more. Supplies were airlifted, instead, from Lyneham. Grove closed about September 1955. Visit it now and extensive house building will be seen to have spread onto the one-time airfield.

Harwell

SU465925. 5 miles S of Abingdon, by A34
Atoms and Arnhem, Wellington and Nun May, energy and excitement, turbine blades and Fairey Battles — not to mention anemometry and Ansons — all have a niche in Harwell's history. Here was sited Britain's prime nuclear research centre. Now it has become a vast, enterprising laboratory. Nuclear physics is here applied for peaceful purposes, and many fields of advanced science and technology are studied. About one half of the research here is nuclear, one-third government inspired technological development, leaving the remainder of effort by the 1,000 or so scientists and engineers to be applied to meet industrial needs.

Research programmes are wide. Geothermal energy harnessing ocean energy by use of wave energy converters, biofuels, automated rail track inspection, lasers for industrial use, submersible robots for underwater inspection of ships, even more highly sophisticated robots, research into ceramics — all and more are featured in Harwell's programmes. Aeronautical association remains, for quality control radiographic inspection, developed for the nuclear power industry, has been applied to running jet engines. Neutron bombardment of RB 211 blades has taken place in the Dido reactor to ensure that cooling fuel can flow freely within the intended blade cavities.

Non-destructive Testing (NDT) found an unusual application when, in 1976, the mechanism of the Great Clock of Westminster, old 'Big Ben', was examined. A welding failure had resulted in the heavy chiming drum being hurled across the clock room, wrecking the chamber mechanism. Harwell's investigation of the clock revealed many further flaws, including one in the hour striking mechanism. Not surprisingly the laboratory's expertise has travelled wide and variously, just as its airmen did four decades previously. As a research establishment Harwell's tasks have been widespread; aeronautically its history provides a microcosm of the history of wartime activity in the central area of England.

Harwell's setting is superb, with the Lambourn Hills stretching from east to west forming the southern rim. A belt of greensand combined with the close proximity of Didcot's rail link with London made fruit farming in the area viable in days gone by. Official requisition of some of the Upper Chalk level countryside was followed by its use as a temporary night landing ground where, in April 1935, it was decided to build an Expansion Period bomber station. Construction of which commenced in June 1935.

Pre-war Battles of 226 Squadron airborne from Harwell. (Ron Clarke.)

Harwell came under RAF control between 2 and 12 February 1937. Two weeks later, *The Times* recorded that Harwell's 220 acres had been purchased for £11,650! In April 1937, No 226 Squadron arrived from Upper Heyford with Hawker Audaxes, with which type No 105 Squadron reformed here on 26 April. Both squadrons used army co-operation aircraft due to bomber shortage.

In June 1937 they were temporarily joined by four squadron's of Avro Ansons, here to participate in the Hendon Display fly-past. On 14 June, Hinds of 107 Squadron moved in from Old Sarum, completing Harwell's bomber complement.

On 18 August 1937, *K7571*, the first Fairey Battle to be based here, arrived for 105 Squadron which equipped fully in September, followed by 226 Squadron in October 1937. Maybe more portentous, was the November sighting of a mushroom on the landing ground.

HM King George VI and the Chief of the Air Staff, Air Chief Marshal Sir Cyril Newall visited Harwell on 9 May 1938. They were received by Air Chief Marshal Sir Edgar Ludlow Hewitt, AOC-in-C, Bomber Command and the AOC 1 Group which controlled Harwell. Considerable interest surrounded the first flight of the Martin Baker MB.2 fighter at Harwell on 3 March 1938.

The Battle squadrons trained realistically and, in August, 107 Squadron received Blenheim Is in time for the Munich crisis. All the Merlin 1 engined Battle 1s of 105 and 226 Squadrons were ordered to be exchanged for Cottesmore's Merlin II Battle IIs of 35 and 207 Squadrons. These non-mobilization squadrons were not earmarked for the AASF where Merlin I spares would not be held and, in October 1938, the switch took place. In winter the airfield became a quagmire. Surface experiments were undertaken using netting and cinders, but only concrete — or better weather — could improve it.

During May 1939, 107 Squadron moved to Wattisham, and Harwell hosted 11,000 pedestrians, 1,100 cars, sixteen 'charabancs' and an unknown number of German spies on Empire Air Day. What they could not have discovered were the station's war plans. They were obvious, though, on 2 September 1939 when the Battles now forming 72 Wing left for France.

The replacement was complete by 17 September 1939 with the arrival of 75 and 148 Squadrons. Under 6 Group's control, Harwell became 3 Group Pool accommodating Wellington Is. Machine gun posts were set-up around the airfield perimeter, likewise at the Q-Site opened on 3 September. Training featured Bomber Command's intention to operate in formation and in daylight.

By January 1940 it was clear that Bomber Command would need to operate principally at night, meaning ample navigation training for which Ansons were already in use. Conversion of some Battle squadrons to Blenheims had already commenced. Whilst it had no direct effect upon Harwell it brought exotic involvement when, on 1 December 1939, with bad weather closing in, a DH 86 *G-ACVY* and a HP 42 *G-AACX* were forced to land, and proceed to France the following day.

Harsh realities from operational experience were related to the Wellington trainees by Wing Commander Griffiths of 99 Squadron. He had participated in the shattering operations of December 1939 and came on 30 January 1940 when it snowed heavily. The cold became intense as Harwell lay deep in snow. Rapid clearing from operational areas had been barely considered, the main means of removal being by hand and shovel. There were numerous reports on 14 February 1940 of a Heinkel 111 in the area, never confirmed nor discounted. It was at about this time that Ryman and Canning devised the 'Harwell boxes' for navigation purposes and these were copied at other stations.

In March 1940 the first Wellington Ias arrived at Harwell after some operational flying with 149 Squadron. On 4 April 1940 both 75 and 148 Squadrons amalgamated, SHQ closed and the whole station was rejuvenated as 15 OTU on 8 April but remained within 6 Group. Its holding of

In that cold, bleak winter of early 1940, a Wellington 1 at Harwell.

Wellingtons and Ansons began increasing, an arrival of 20 May being Wellington 1 *L4265* ex-149 Squadron and one which operated against Brunsbuttel's shipping on 4 September 1939. It was eventually lost without trace on 18 March 1942 whilst flying a training exercise.

Action in Norway then France resulted in an expansion of operational training. It also brought, on 24 May 1940, the first operational diversion to Harwell, a Whitley of 77 Squadron flown by Pilot Officer Mahaddie, later of pathfinder fame. Increased flying meant more accidents such as when an Anson, *N5186* crashed in flames in a field near the bomb dump, killing the pilot, Wing Commander Hughes.

Operational flying by 15 OTU commenced on the night of 18-19 July 1940 when three Wellingtons dropped leaflets over the Dunkirk-Boulogne area. On 23-24 July three more crossed the Channel to Amiens, Cherbourg and Rouen. Dieppe, Evreux, Beauvais and Caen were visited on 27-28 July. Such activity was reckoned good for crews and recipients.

During the afternoon of 14 August some 20 Whitleys arrived from Driffield to make Harwell their point of departure and return during a long haul to Milan and back that night. Luckily they had left by the time the station received its first bombing attack, around 18:00 on 16 August. The raider swept in over Rowstock and dropped four bombs. Two 400 gallon petrol bowsers caught fire, one being towed away most courageously. Three Wellingtons were destroyed and

The NAAFI and Sergeants' Mess at Harwell. (UK AEA.)

two out of seven casualties were fatal. Machine-gunning was responsible for casualties and damage. Poor station defences amounted to a few twin Vickers gun emplacements and a 3 ton Beford lorry mounting twin Vickers guns on a Scarff ring.

Soon after midnight a further six bombs were aimed at 15 OTU, leaving neither damage nor casualties. Later that day Harwell was told to disperse aircraft and use the satellite at Hampstead placing some AA defences there because large scale night attacks were forecast for the coming moon period. The Luftwaffe had far from finished with Harwell and during the afternoon of 19 August a Ju 88 strafed and bombed the stations destroying a further three Wellingtons. A short respite was followed by yet another

attack on 26 August when bombs fell near the bomb dump. The casualties amounted to six RAF and ten civilians. That night six of Dishforth's Whitleys operated from Harwell.

These were indeed difficult days, but despite the enemy interference, and the constant invasion fears when Ansons stood ready each with 2 × 112 lb bombs, 15 OTU managed 1,594 daylight and 665 night hours of flying training, its force of fifty Wellingtons and seventeen Ansons resulting in a better pupil output than larger units in 6 Group. There were many accidents, though, especially at night. Undercarriage collapse after a heavy landing was frequent, and there were bent wings, too, for night flying from grass was often hazardous. The runway was marked by about ten or so goose-necked

Harwell's domestic site. The MT section is in the left hand corner with barrack blocks, Sergeants' Mess and NAAFI central. Married quarters are in the distance. (UK AEA.)

flares, long spouted cans of paraffin fitted with thick wicks and placed so that the wind blew the flame away from the fuel reservoir. From time to time aircraft would knock them over. In addition to the lights of Harwell there were those of the large Didcot railway installation which distracted more than one pupil pilot.

In the building, now the Plastics' Technology Building, there was a bombing teacher and a Wellington fuselage for training purposes so that crews could become familiar with the aircraft's layout. Another trainer was devoted to radio aids, in all a very primitive type of flight simulator.

Summer 1940 was a desperate period, with staff and trainees expecting the call to repel an invasion. Three Wellingtons went *Nickelling* on 7 September in a sort of defiant gesture. If any crews worried about balloon cables they could take comfort when, on 18 September 1940, *L4322* returned safely after colliding with a cable over Yeovil. Six more *Nickel* sorties were flown, over three nights, in October 1940.

That the enemy was still around was clear on 13 November when Ju 88, *L1 + LS*, Werke Nr *6557* of LG1, which had flown across Oxfordshire, was damaged by Spitfires of 611 Squadron and crashed at Blewbury. Three of the crew were captured and taken to Didcot. The fourth was buried at Harwell on 19 November.

King Haakon of the Norwegians visited the station on 12 December. He was treated to a fly past by three Ansons one of which shed part of a cowling when pulling too steeply out of a dive. Another disaster came on 26 March 1941. Sergeant Mowntney and crew were detailed to take *R1243* along the Worcester–Harlech–Peterborough track, then return to Harwell. En route they were to attack sea markers in Cardigan Bay using smoke floats. As they entered the training area they inadvertantly raced into sea fog. From Criccieth their aircraft was seen to hit the sea 1½ miles offshore. Boats were launched and two men rescued, one of whom died. Of the other four there was no further trace.

March brought two attacks on the station's Q-Site and defences were now at high alert as proved on 5 March. Harwell's Anson N5078 was twelve miles north of Banbury at 20:45 when it became coned by searchlights which refused to extinguish even when the recognition signal was flashed. Therefore the aircraft's captain decided to fire the Very light colour of the day. Unfortunately the pistol discharged within the aircraft which was set ablaze forcing the crew to bale out fast.

Early on 11 April 1941 the enemy came again to Harwell. After circling, a raider dived and released two bombs, repeated the action and machine-gunned the station. A crew, walking between two hangars, thought they saw a cat run by. In fact it was a bomb bouncing along the tarmac which came to rest at the solid fuel dump without exploding. Another went through the superstructure on the west side of what is now Hangar 8 and came to rest unexploded under a starter trolley at the northeast corner of Hangar 9. A third bomb exploded by Hangar 2 (now No 8) while the fourth rested by the water tower. In 1946 a member of the Nuclear Physics Division dashed into Building 30 to announce that a bomb was lodged in No 8 Hangar roof. However all was well — it was the tail unit of one of April's delivery of five years earlier.

Nickelling continued into 1941, the twentieth operation being mounted on 6-7 May. Harwell life was abruptly changed when Group HQ despatched a signal on 30 April to the effect that 15 OTU must train 15 crews monthly each of which would ferry a Wellington to the Near East. Ferrying had previously been undertaken by 3 Group squadrons who started out from Stradishall. The pattern now was for the aircraft involved to be collected from Overseas Air Delivery Flight Kemble by 15 OTU, and for departure to take place from Hampstead Norris from where the first three left on 9-10 May 1941. On 24 May the commitment was raised to twelve crews a fortnight from the OTU, ten for ferry duty and overseas service.

June 1941 found 15 OTU the busiest in 6 Group. During 3,040 flying hours there had been fourteen flying accidents and the output was ninety pilots, forty observers and eighty radio operator/air gunners, roughly a quarter of the entire Group output.

News arrived on 18 July which would lead to a much improved Harwell status. Upon that day the decision was made to lay two runways of 1,100 yds and one of 1,000 yds. The station was therefore declared non-operational with effect from 21 July 1941, this halting Nickelling until 14 October when six Wellingtons carried out Operation No 34 to central France from where R1275 and R1783 failed to return. The OTU had placed its A and B Flights at Mount Farm on 24 July and moved its ferrying sections to Hampstead on 28 July. Flying did not entirely cease at Harwell for, while the flare path was lit, it was twice attacked on 20 September. During that month 15 OTU flew 3,367 hours.

Harwell reopened, with McAlpine's concrete runways almost completed, on 23 November 1941. The Lorenz beam lined up with the main runway helped to maintain regular winter flying, for which Grove was to be available if ready in time.

During February 1942 the 50th Course passed out. Overseas deliveries by 15 OTU were continuing. Twenty Wellingtons set off from Harwell on the Cologne 1,000 bomber raid and two did not return. For the Essen raid 21 took off and safely returned. Bremen was attacked by eleven out of nineteen Wellingtons despatched on 25-26 June and two were lost. Harwell participated in Grand Nationals (Main Force bombing operations) after which OTUs concentrated upon training — instead of operations.

The main flying accidents became

memorable. In 1942 *X3209* tried a night take off, carrying a full fuel and bomb load. Half way along the runway the bomber slewed on its belly into contractor's excavations. The starboard engine burst into fierce flames whilst the crew remained inside the aircraft, too severely shocked even to leave. Wing Commander Dabinett, close by, raced to the aircraft and switched off the fuel flow, then the fire crew tackled the blaze, knowing that the aircraft had bombs aboard.

Another memorable incident involved *T2557*, returning to Harwell on 21 August 1942. Its night flight about ended, the Wellington suddenly rammed into a Chipping Norton Oxford. Both showered down, a mass of flames, on to the town. Four nights later a further mid-air collision occurred. *DV595*, night flying from Harwell, collided with *N2775*, operating from Hampstead Norris and lining up for Stanton Harcourt. They collided over Odstone Bombing Range, the pilot of *N2775*

regaining control for a single-engine crash landing at Stanton. *DV595* came down near Uffington.

During summer 1942 some overseas delivery flights started from Harwell, many adventures overtaking their crews. *W5565* made an eight-hour flight from Harwell to Gibraltar in daylight on 8 November 1942, then headed along the west African coast towards Bathurst but never arrived. Pilot Officer A. B. Kidson and crew had been shot down near Dakar by French fighters. In September 1942, 25 Wellingtons left Harwell for a new departure point. Portreath. Of these nineteen reached Gibraltar. One later force landed off Sicily.

Bombing raids on Italy in late 1942 attracted bombers to use Harwell as an advanced base. On 20-21 November nine Wellingtons of 420 and five of 425 Squadrons left from here for Turin. Next night they flew mining sorties. Both squadrons repeated these operations later that month. On 7 January 1943

View north-west across Harwell on 20 July 1942 showing dispersed Wellingtons of 15 OTU and camouflaged runways. (RAF Museum.)

Lancaster *W4330* of 460 Squadron became the first of its type to be diverted here.

Like others, No 15 OTU participated in *Bullseye*, and resumed *Nickelling* on 4 December 1942. Night diversions increased, as on 17-18 January when eight Lancasters (five of 97 Squadron, one of 50 Squadron and two of 1660 Heavy Conversion Unit) landed from Berlin. 'Q' of 1660 HCU had hydraulic failure, preventing the bomb doors from opening. The load remained aboard when the aircraft landed. A Lancaster of 50 Squadron from Dusseldorf arrived on 23 January. It had been intercepted by a Bf 110 which injured the mid-upper gunner.

Wellington deliveries continued into 1943; fourteen setting fourth in January, twenty in February. Control of the operation was by 1443 Ferry Training Flight. The 73rd OTU course passed out on 27 February. A new flying control building (now containing Harwell's General Administration Department) opened on 17 February 1943 as a flying and operations control centre. Watch was kept from there over the departure of forty Wellingtons overseas as well as two *Nickelling* operations in March.

Increased sophistication failed to prevent accidents. Wellington 1c *X3171*, on a solo cross country flight, crashed mid-afternoon on 1 March in Northumberland and the crew died. On 3 March, *HF906*, practising overshoots from Hampstead Norris, was overtaken by power setting problems, then smashed into cottages at Common Barn, near Hermitage. Its crew, two civilians and livestock were killed. Another fatal accident involving one of 15 OTU's first Wellington IIIs occurred on 11 March and, on April 3, two Wellingtons collided during circuit flying. Such an event remained unusual despite the intense activity. The risks increased during fighter affiliation and it was all too easy for a Martinet to get out of control as happened on 11 May. Another problem was selection of the correct runway at the right airfield. On 19 May 1943, Wellington *HZ437* of 310 Ferry Training Unit, which emerged from 1443 FTF in April 1943, crashed two miles from Turweston. The wrong runway was approached and close to landing the pilot realized his error. With insufficient speed to go round again the bomber spun in.

Mediterranean departures continued from Harwell, 39 in April, 33 in May, seven in June. Operational involvement remained as in late June 1943 when Wellingtons carried out mining. *Nickelling* and *Bullseyes* continued into 1944. Overseas delivery flights ended in October 1943 and the FTU disbanded on 17 December 1943. Still mainly equipped with Wellington 1cs, 15 OTU periodically flew ASR searches. December found 15 OTU re-equipping with Wellington Xs whose stay was short for, on 3 March 1944, the OTU closed.

Displaying a changed role, Harwell reopened on 1 April 1944 within 38 Group, Airborne Forces. Two Albemarle squadrons arrived, Nos 295 and 570, and with them a host of Horsa gliders, sufficient for Harwell's participation in Exercise *Dreme* on 4 April. Next night ten Albemarles flew *Nickel* sorties over France and another seven on 10 April. A night navigation training tour was laid on, also more sorties over France. In Exercise *Posh*, two Albemarles of 570 Squadron acting as pathfinders, practised their part in the Normandy landings by dropping twenty troops and supplies at Winterbourne Stoke. Another three practised at Tarrant Rushton. Similar, larger exercises followed in rapid succession.

An interesting diversion was provided on 23 May by the first flight of the very fast Martin Baker MB.5 fighter, but the invasion training was paramount. By the end of May all was ready for Harwell's vital contribution to the Normandy invasion. One hour before midnight on 5 June 1944, three Albemarles from each squadron took off to spearhead *Tonga*. Each dropped ten men to set up *Rebecca* beacons to guide the main force. Another twelve Albemarles brought part of the main paratroop force, and a further 28 towed Horsas, one carrying General Gale and Divisional HQ.

Crews then rested before Operation

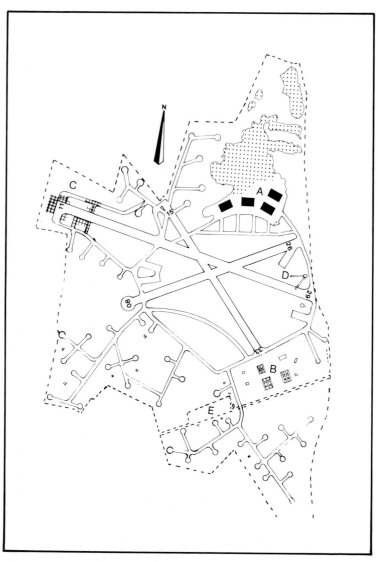

Harwell in 1945 exhibited the worst features of an OTU. The runways intersected closely making them vulnerable to bombing and highly inducive to flying accidents. The extraordinary layout of the perimeter tracking and taxi tracks, even to the extent of additional tracks leading to the hangar apron, is very obvious. The weapons dump **B** was dangerously placed at the end of the runway—the shortest runway. Glider marshalling tracked area can be seen at **C**. **D** marks the position of the unusual catapult station and **E** a civilian held farm—in no small way a hazardous position! **A** and the shaded area is the technical site.

Mallard, the towing of loaded Horsas to Normandy in which 38 Harwell combinations took part. Special Operations Executive supply drops and further training followed. Albemarles were only stop-gap glider tugs used until sufficient four-engined aircraft were available. Harwell's first Stirling IV arrived on 14 June, and a count of the aircraft available on 11 July showed 64 Albemarles, nineteen Stirlings and eighty Horsas. Night SOE drop operations using Stirlings began on 27 July and continued spasmodically until early September 1944 and the next airborne assault. Before then the enemy briefly counter-attacked, using a V-1 flying bomb which arrived on 30 August destroying three grounded aircraft.

An airborne attack supporting a Rhine crossing finalized as Operation *Market*, was ordered for 17 September 1944. Shortly after 11:00, Stirlings of 295 and 570 Squadrons set off leading a giant cavalcade to Arnhem. By mid-afternoon all the Stirlings were safely home. Ground crews prepared more gliders for the morrow, a misty day forcing delay of Phase II. Later, thirteen Stirlings towed off Horsas and another 32 carried containers for the ground forces. Resupply of the Arnhem force became a vital, daily task with flak taking a steady toll of the aircraft. Misty mornings delayed the operations for which extensive fighter cover was essential because the transports could little vary their routing. On 20 September fighter cover failed but Harwell's squadrons did not suffer as badly as others.

The enormity of the Arnhem failure was then clear and final supply drops took place on 23 September. Fighter ground support was poor and AA guns brought down four of 570 Squadron's Stirlings. A further two had to force land. Barely had Harwell's squadrons licked their wounds when they were ordered to Rivenhall, Essex. A further stage in Harwell's history was about to unfold.

On 12 October it again hosted an OTU, No 13 under Air Defence of Great Britain and 12 Group and the training centre for 2 Group TAF crews. Fighter-bomber Mosquito crews were to train here, but this was altered when 60 OTU merged with 13 OTU on 1 March 1945. Mosquitoes were placed at Finmere, 13 OTU's satellite, and at Hampstead Norris. Aircraft of 60 OTU arrived at both satellites on 15 March, and at long last 13 OTU became part of 2 Group. Harwell had housed 13 OTU's Mitchells and Bostons, flying of the latter ceasing on 19 March. Harwell then held the Mitchell Wing, its strength at the end of April 1945 being sixty Mitchells, seven Spitfires and an Anson.

The last Mitchell course completed training on 28 May and 13 OTU contracted. Late July 1945 it moved to Middleton St George. On 22 July, Harwell and its two satellites returned to 38 Group, the satellites being placed on Care and Maintenance. A party from the School of Air Transport arrived on 27 July but, the airfield being unready for them, they returned to Netheravon. On 21 August the School of Flight Efficiency, Transport Command, moved in followed by the Transport Command Development Unit from Netheravon on 1 September. Delay had been occasioned by work on the runway intersection.

Barely had the units settled when they were told that Harwell was passing to the Ministry of Supply and becoming a centre for atomic research. RAF units moved to Brize Norton on 14 December 1945 and the Service vacated the station on 31 December.

A British atomic bomb had first been suggested in March 1940. By the end of 1942 resources and safety were more available in America to where the work was switched. By autumn of 1944 it was obvious that Britain needed a post-war nuclear experimental establishment, the question being — where should it be? Airfields offered space, workshops, roads, water and power facilities and hangars to house the nuclear plant. Close proximity to a major university — the Clarendon or Cavendish Laboratories, at Oxford or Cambridge — was necessary.

Air Ministry listed seventeen airfields which they were prepared to release, mostly with limited facilities. Preference among scientists was for a site near

Cambridge with which many had associations, but Air Ministry was not keen. East Anglian airfields would retain strategic importance. When the Ministry was pressed, Duxford and Debden were offered. Radio active waste was then to be buried on site, so a low water table was essential, also ample water supply. Debden, with a high water table, was rejected, Duxford on account of its poor water supply. Benson was considered, then Harwell. Here, the scientists decided, was a most suitable area for

development. Service personnel not pleased to lose their pre-war baronial estate, were given Brize Norton to keep them happy whilst Sir John Cockcroft and his team confirmed their choice — in the nearby *Horse and Jockey*.

The area and facilities seemed suitable and communications were good. Perhaps with similar feelings Air Ministry produced reasons why they should not release the station. Its long runways could be used for Brabazon flying, they claimed, then the Thames Conservancy

A 1946 view of Harwell showing one of the Type 'C' Aircraft Sheds and Workshops (Type 2048-2049/1934) in the foreground.

expressed concern about effluent discharge. Eventually it was agreed, Harwell it must be. On 1 January 1946 the scientists took control.

A stupendous future lay before Harwell, study ranging from particle physics to large reactors. Nuclear fuels would be studied, also the production of radio isotopes for medical and industrial purposes.

By the mid-1950s, Harwell had 94 buildings, only 34 from RAF days. The large 'C' Type hangars would be used for purposes far beyond anything their originators had in mind, one now housing a large reactor. By 1957 the Atomic Energy Research Establishment had grown quite vast, so parts were hived off. The National Institute for Research into Nuclear Sciences used the original Harwell buildings. On an adjacent site was the Rutherford Laboratory under the control of the Science Research Council. In 1959 at Winfrith a new site was built to explore power reactor development. Fusion research would now be studied at

The Atomic Energy Research Establishment, Harwell, can be seen here to be utilizing many of the former RAF station's buildings. (UK AEA.)

The last aircraft to land at Harwell, T-33A 18756 of the 514th Fighter Interceptor Wing, Manston, which forced landed in January 1956. (UK AEA.)

Inside the Dido Reactor at Harwell. Prominent is the Dido rig flask for changing fuel rods, and being positioned by a travelling crane. (UK AEA.)

Culham Laboratory whilst at Grove airfield research was to take place into industrial applications of isotopes until this task returned to Harwell in the 1970s. A more recent off-shoot from AERE has been a Medical Research Council unit researching into the protection of human tissues from radiation. AERE employs about three-quarters of the Harwell workforce.

Flying did not cease in January 1946, for there was an alarming episode some years later. A USAF T-33 jet trainer in trouble mistook Harwell's closed runway for an active one and landed. Once down, could it leave? RATO bottles were strapped in place and the intrepid pilot tried. Alas, the aeroplane just could not make it.

Although much work here is connected with technological development, one inevitably associates Harwell with atomic physics. For the uninitiated in a nuclear environment there is a sense of foreboding and concern at what takes place unseen. A visitor to the Dido reactor first views a model of a fuel cell along with cutaway and sectional drawings. Plastic shoe coverings are donned before entering the reactor area within which many of its functions are recorded and observed in a control room. From an upper gallery one can see the apparatus needed to remove a fuel cell from the reactor which requires the rod to be encased, mechanically of course, in a lead container.

Kelmscot

SU240980. 2½ miles SE of Lechlade
Immediately north of Kelmscot village, land was requisitioned for an 'L'-shaped landing ground. It had further strange characteristics for, in its prime of life, it attracted only eleven buildings in a small group on its north-west side. They included one Over Type Blister hangar (12512/41), a dining and recreation hut and two Handcraft Type airmens' barrack huts (2886/42). A 36 ft × 16 ft Nissen hut stood by a dispersal and another (10024/ 41) served as a control tower. Kelmscot, Watchfield's RLG, was used for beam approach training.

Two miles east of the Faringdon-Barford road was the outer marker, an inner marker being sited at the threshold to No 1 Flying Lane. The main beacon lay west of the landing strip. There were no runways in the usual sense, but instead a flying lane (vector 09/27) or grass landing strip 1,400 yards long and 50 yards wide. Two other very short flying lanes were roughly orientated north/ south and north-west/south-east. The long lane was used by Oxford pilots practising blind approach techniques. For this purpose Kelmscot came into use on 17 October 1942, remaining on hand for No 1 Blind Approach School until the end of 1946.

It knew one other period of different usage. For a week in May 1944 it was closed to flying and used as a dropping zone for paratroops brought overhead in Dakotas of 46 Group. These drops, last minute preparations for the Normandy assault, commenced on 7 May 1944 with Exercise *Noggin*, an early morning drop of the 1st Polish Parachute Brigade, from eighteen of Down Ampney's Dakotas. On 8 May fifty Dakotas in Exercise *Nark* - ten from each of five squadrons — brought troops of the 1st Polish Brigade in greater number. Release was lower and in one case from an aircraft too low. As a result a stick of paratroops overshot the DZ incurring casualties, four of which were fatal.

In Exercise *Noggin II* on 10 May fifty Dakotas delivered troops of the 2nd Polish Brigade. On the following day Exercise *Nark II* took place here. This time 49 Dakotas provided the airlift in addition to which five acted as pathfinders. Operating from Down Ampney, the troops were again of the 2nd Polish Brigade, Exercise *Nark III* mounted on 12 May comprised 27 Dakotas and two pathfinders, the aircraft being drawn from Nos 48, 233 and 271 Squadrons. These were relatively small exercises compared with some others, but made good use of Kelmscot which could, briefly, be said to be taking a part in the invasion preparations.

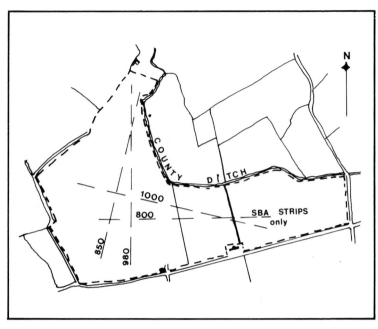

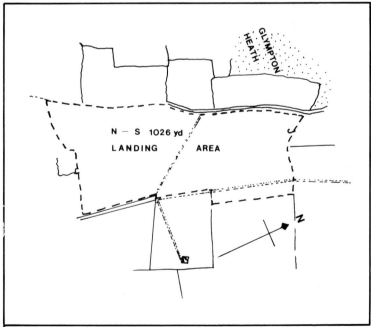

Above left *Kelmscot was a most unusual airfield in that it served as a Relief Landing Ground for the Beam Approach School at Watchfield. As it was approach training that was mostly undertaken, no permanent accommodation for personnel was provided. There was, however, a temporary Enlarged Over Blister hangar here. Shown on the diagram are the grass strip runs available and their lengths in yards.*

Below left *Kiddington was a small Relief Landing Ground, a grass strip without hangars and with no accommodation for personnel.*

Kiddington (also known as Glympton)

SP438230. 5 miles NW of Woodstock, off A34, 1 mile NE of Glympton

Kiddington's RLG opened near Glympton in the summer of 1940, and Harvards and Oxfords of 15 SFTS used the field in 1940–41. Further use was made by Kiddington's glider OTU's in 1942. Early in 1943 it came under 20 (P) AFU which used it, spasmodically, until June 1945.

Kidlington

SP475153. 6 miles NW of Oxford by A34(T)

Kidlington has a more varied history than most city airports, wartime expansion into a rectangular array of huts and roads bringing it into line with training establishments. It came into use in 1938, No 26 Elementary and Reserve Flying Training School masterminded by Marshall of Cambridge opening here on 24 June. First to arrive was Audax K7552, the School's strength increasing to include Tiger Moths, Audaxes and Hinds before its closure at the outbreak of war. By that time Air Training (Oxford) was using two Tipsy Trainers (G-AFRV and G-AFVN) for its part in the Civil Air Guard Scheme.

On 9 September 1939 Fairey Battles of 52 Squadron dispersed here for a few days for Kidlington had become Abingdon's satellite. They left when their parent unit moved to Benson, Kidlington then coming under 4 Group Pool, Abingdon.

Late 1939 control passed to 6 SFTS, Little Rissington. That station became waterlogged and, on 8 January 1940, E and G Flights of 6 SFTS, along with F and H servicing parties and the Advanced Training Squadron HQ, moved to Kidlington. The latter became unusable following heavy snow on 27 January. Barely was it fully serviceable when, in mid-March, it had to close again.

Kidlington then became an RLG under 6 SFTS until that unit abruptly withdrew its complement in mid-August 1940. Bombing of Brize Norton caused a rapid dispersal, half of the ITS, 15 SFTS, and ground staff quickly moving into Kidlington on 19 August 1940 to reduce the large number of vulnerable aircraft at Brize Norton. 6 MU also used Kidlington — still a rudimentary site although major expansion had started. Air Training (Oxford) had two hangars in which they had switched from their pre-war flying school activity to undertaking aircraft overhaul. Campsfield House was requisitioned for dormitory use. The movement of 15 SFTS from Brize Norton increased Kidlington's importance within 23 Group. Then on 31 August 1940, the remainder of ITS 15 SFTS arrived from South Cerney where it had lodged when Middle Wallop became a fighter station. A count on 31 August 1940 showed that Kidlington held 56 Harvard 1s and two Oxfords.

Headquarters' staff of 15 SFTS arrived on 1 October 1940, the remainder of 15 SFTS following on 17 October, with over 100 Harvards on charge and wartime building well advanced. On 1 November 1940, 15 SFTS acquired Weston-on-the-Green as its second RLG.

Need for ample dispersal was audible at 15:15 on 3 November 1940. In low cloud and rain, a Ju 88 swept in from the north east and raced low over the technical site and dropped five bombs. One ricochetted its way through the station armoury and another hit a hangar before bouncing back into the armoury and

Kidlington from the air on 21 August 1940. (PRO.)

exploding. Two others burst on the landing ground where the fifth rested unexploded. The Ju 88, machine guns blazing, scurried into cloud flying south-westerly. One person was killed, two seriously injured. The armoury and Hangar 4, along with an Air Training Co hangar, were all seriously damaged, and two Harvards burnt.

Throughout the winter of 1940–41 Harvards and Oxfords used Kidlington. On 27 February another Ju 88 appeared, flying at around 300 ft along the Woodstock road. A Kidlington gun post crew opened fire and, returning it, the raider retreated.

Surface state was hindering flying so,

on 28 February 1941, a Flight from 15 SFTS moved to Watton. On 8 March use of that operational station increased when two separate Flights, each of five aircraft, moved there for flying training. The need for detachments was alleviated when, on 30 June 1941, a new RLG, at Barford, opened.

A switch from Harvards to Oxfords took place over several weeks, at the start of 1941 and Oxford flying training continued throughout 1941. Concern that winter would bring a poor surface resulted in the start of runway laying in autumn 1941. On 23 December, with the customary two Sommerfeld track runways available, Oxfords of J and K Flights

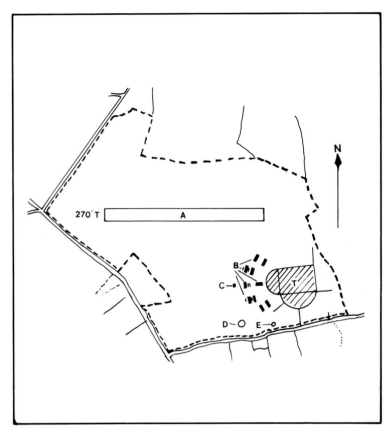

The late war layout of Kidlington included an Army Track runway (1,200 yd long, 50 yd wide) marked **A** *on the plan. The eight hangars marked* **B** *included seven Bellman type and one Horace. Around the perimeter were up to ten 65 ft Blister hangars.* **C** *Control tower* **D** *The 30 ft compass swinging pad for use by Oxfords* **E** *The 15 ft compass pad* **T** *Technical and administrative site.*

15 SFTS returned from Weston, forced out because 2 GTS formed there. On the day after their arrival a letter reached Kidlington confirming that 15 SFTS was to close. A new 'No 15', called 15 (P) AFU, was to form at Leconfield in January 1942. Intake at 15 SFTS ceased, but courses completed flying programmes and Oxfords of the School continued to fly from here until 11 April 1942.

On 1 January 1942, No 1 Glider OTU controlled by 70 Group formed at Kidlington, for after a GTS course a pilot would acquire operational skills at an OTU. Before this scheme became effective, the Horsa had been selected as the assault glider and the Hotspur relegated to training duties. A few OTUs were formed, a glider pilot after leaving GTS finding himself flying a Hotspur towed by an antique Hector as before. A second glider OTU formed at Kidlington in February 1942, and both were renamed 101 and 102 OTUs soon after. They functioned until June 1942 when the HGCU opened at Shrewton.

From Kidlington a party proceeded to Shobden on 28 May to form 5 GTS. Then, on 13 July, the remaining Hotspur organization and SHQ Kidlington combined to form 4 GTS. Kidlington had lost its RLG at Barford St John on 10 April and now switched to using Kingston Bagpuize. No 4 GTS retained Kidlington as its busy home until it amalgamated with Nos 1 and 2 GTSs to form an entirely new unit, No 20 (P) AFU, an entirely new unit, on 10 March 1943. Equipped with Oxfords it made use until November 1944, of Croughton. Flying also took place from Kiddington and Hinton-in-the-Hedges before disbandment on 21 June 1945. A non-flying unit then formed at Kidlington, No 1 Aircrew Holding Unit, and stayed until September 1945. No 265 MU was also here and at Grove between October 1945 and 1948.

After the war the Oxford Aeroplane Club formed. In 1959 considerable expansion commenced after the Oxford UAS which had been here since 1949 departed. Kidlington became an outlet for Piper aircraft and in 1961 the first Commercial Pilot Licence students arrived for training, and British Executive Air Services, part of Pressed Steel, ran courses leading to Private Pilot Licence standard. The Oxford school in May 1964 became the first to be CAA approved for the training of CPL students. Eventually it evolved into the Oxford Air Training School.

Kidlington's present control tower was built in 1964-65, an upper room being added in 1969-70. Some wartime buildings remain, including the Officer's Mess, complete with frontal drive and small lawn. A dome trainer also survives. Kidlington is an active airfield with a variety of civil aircraft coming and going.

By comparison, Kidlington, alias Oxford Airport, in the 1980s. Its aircraft are placed to form the initials of Oxford Air Training School. (Via Squadron Leader G. M. Phillips, MBE.)

Kingston Bagpuize

SU410965. 5 miles SW of Abingdon, S of A415

Kingston Bagpuize, on flat land south of the village, had excellent approaches. Between January and May 1942, 3 EFTS used Kingston as an RLG, then from 9 March 1942 to 19 July 1942 it served as a satellite for 1 GTS Thame whose

Kingston Bagpuize was never completed, its Pierced Steel Planking runways (one 2,000 yd long and two of 1,400 yd) being removed in the autumn of 1944. **A** *'T2' hangar* **B** *Control Tower* **C** *Administration and Technical Site* **D** *Domestic sites. At one time the airfield also hosted two Butler hangars and two large and one small Blister hangars. Accommodation was for a total of 2,974 men.*

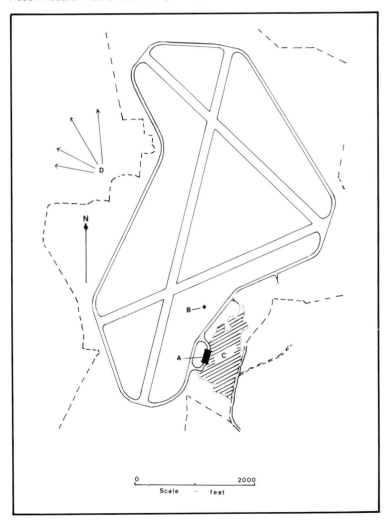

Scale — feet

Hotspurs and tugs undertook circuit training. When a glider pilot refresher school for those trained already and not flying very much was suggested, Kingston and indeed Thame were considered. Nothing came of this and, between January and April 1943, Kingston was used by 4 GTS. On 10 March 1943 it became a satellite of 20 (P) AFU whose Oxfords operated from here. No 20 (P) AFU withdrew on 28 July 1943, plans to enlarge the airfield being then implemented.

When a 70 Group party arrived on 30 January 1944 to take over from the contractors, they found that the USAAF had already moved in. On 7 February 1944 an advance party of IXth AF also arrived. American interest was not so much in operating from the station as in trying a wire mesh covering on the original runway surface. The Commander IXth AF came to inspect this on 10 March, observing rapid refuelling and rearming of 50 P-47s from the 368th Fighter Group, Greenham. Next day the Group mounted three operations from here, testing the efficiency of the novel runway surface. They again used Kingston on 13 April 1944.

An intensive day's flying to test the runway further came on 6 May 1944 when P-47s repeatedly landed showing that frequent repairs were necessary. A B-17, short of fuel, visited briefly on 25 May, and on 15 June circuits by C-47s trying out the runway showed little wear on its surface. Late in June 1944 the experimental wire mesh was removed, all trial work being deemed complete by August 1944. Kingston lay dormant until 14 December 1944 when 3 MU took over the site. The sub-site which 3 MU had established was eventually closed on 14 June 1954.

Mount Farm

SU578963. E of Berrisfield, by A423(T), 8 miles SE of Oxford
Ground purchased for Benson's satellite became known as Mount Farm. Battles of 12 OTU began using the airfield in July 1940 for initial flying training by day and night. There was no fixed accommodation, troops guarding the site using tents.

Following the attack on Stanton Harcourt, a few light machine guns came to protect Mount Farm which, by mid-August, because of its good situation, was already undergoing major development. Concrete runways were being rapidly constructed in the hope that they would be ready in mid-September 1940. Completion was retarded and it was two months later before the runways were fully open.

Policy changes relating to satellites had come about. Now they were for dispersing aircraft and, in September 1940, for reducing bottle necks arising in night flying because of enemy interference with training programmes. Long outdated, the Fairey Battle was now to be phased out, its place taken temporarily by Wellingtons of 12 OTU. Benson's grass surface had stood the tempo of wartime training suprisingly well, but was unsuitable for Wellington night flying training. Mount Farm's runways, on the other hand, were suitable for day and night flying Wellingtons. Extension of these by 300 yds was ordered, when feasible.

On 1 December 1940, 12 OTU was reduced from a Battle armed OTU to a half strength Wellington OTU, flying from Mount Farm and Benson. The reason for reduced strength was the decision to place the PRU at Benson in December 1940. January 1941 found 12 OTU training Wellington crews, a task briefly interrupted in the early afternoon on 27 February 1941 when an enemy bomber, using low cloud cover, penetrated the Benson area. It dropped two bombs about half a mile from Mount Farm whose LAA guns fired unsuccessfully as the raider hastened off to bomb Benson. A second attack, during night flying, resulted in thirteen 50 kg bombs being dropped on Mount Farm. One cratered the north-east/south-west runway and two burst on the peritrack. An NCO was killed, three men injured and damage caused to two Wellingtons and a Magister. A third attack came on 12 May 1941 when a large bomb caused a 50 ft diameter crater, again on the main runway, which was further damaged by a smaller bomb. Another bomb fell on the perimeter track and 15 on waste ground. Such attacks were more of an annoyance than a major disaster.

The prime role continued until the OTU moved to Chipping Warden. Then 15 OTU Harwell took control of Mount Farm, on 23 July 1941, making it a second satellite. Just how fully fledged Mount Farm was at this time could be seen by operational diversions here, nine Hampdens of 61, 106, 144 and 408 Squadrons and two Wellingtons of 218 Squadron on 10 July 1941, returning from attacks on Aachen and Osnabruck.

On 5 September 1941, Benson received No 1416 Flight which became 140 Squadron on September 17 1941. It was mainly equipped with PR Spitfires, and a handful of Blenheims for night reconnaissance. To accommodate PR aircraft, Benson re-possessed Mount Farm in January 1942, 140 Squadron placing four of its Spitfires there on 23 January 1942. Operations continued from Benson. In the event of a German invasion of Britain, 140 Squadron would have mounted a visual and photographic watch upon it, for which reason 140 Squadron had a higher establishment than PR squadrons.

Mount Farm served as a dispersal airfield for Benson's PR Spitfires until 4 May 1942 when both A and B Flights of 140 Squadron moved here whilst Benson's concrete runways were built. Into Mount Farm came up to ten PR Spitfires, variously known as Mk 5, Type 'F,' 'G' and Mk 1a along with six Blenheim IVs and a Tiger Moth. From Mount Farm the Blenheims flew night reconnaissance flights, using photo flashes for photography. Spitfires flew daylight PR sorties over France. The Dieppe landing was being prepared, that area becoming much photographed by 140 Squadron. After postponement, a second busy period came in the run-up to the raid. Between 15 and 22 August 1942, 63 of the 75 Spitfire sorties were successfully flown, many to Dieppe. On 17 August 1942, a busy day when the squadron flew 22 Spitfire sorties, many

covered Dieppe among them R7115, flown by Pilot Officer L. G. Smith who flew six runs across the port and obtained pictures from 30,000 ft.

Blenheim operations became increasingly dangerous. Twice towards the end of June 1942 crews reported seeing night fighters, and Blenheim sorties ended with a night reconnaissance to the Cherbourg Peninsula on 15 August 1942.

On 15 March 1943, 140 Squadron moved to Hartford Bridge and Mount Farm's future immediately changed.

During the USAAF tenure at Mount Farm Lockheed P-38s and their photo-reconnaissance derivatives could be seen at the base.

B

D

D

D

D

WAAF

D

T

B

T

D

D

Mount Farm, despite its early war completion and importance never had more than eight Blister hangars **B**, four 65 ft Over type and four of the 69 ft Enlarged Over style. Runways had asphalt surfaces. Note the two types of hardstandings. The round type are the early ones and the small pads **C** for fighter-type aircraft. **D** Domestic sites **T** Technical sites.

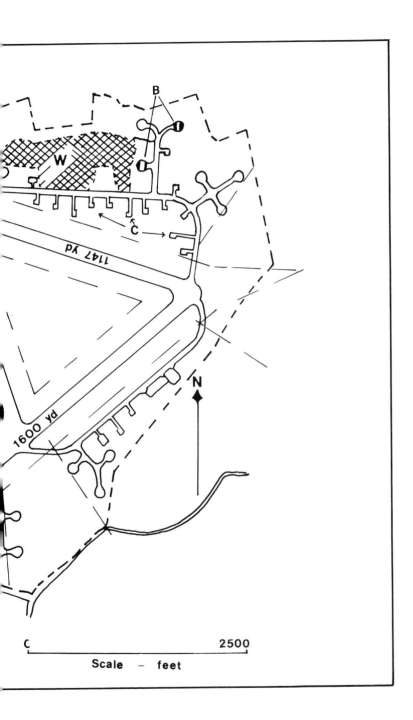

B

W

1147 yd

C

1600 yd

N

C   2500

Scale — feet

Gearing up for a tactical PR role was the 13th PR Squadron, USAAF which arrived at Podington on 2 December 1942 and was awaiting an operational base. Mount Farm provided it and, on 16 February 1943, the 13th Photographic Squadron arrived, bringing some L-4 Piper Cubs, although it was mainly equipped with P-38 and F-5 Lightnings. During 1943 reverse Lend-Lease Spitfires played an ever increasing part in the squadron's equipment and were used to obtain target and damage assessment photographs for 8th AAF Bomb Groups.

Second to arrive was the 14th PR Squadron (Light) on 12 May 1943. It operated P-38s, F-4s and F-5s and later Spitfires. The 22nd Photographic Squadron (Light) reached Mount Farm 8 June 1943 and also equipped with P-38s and Spitfires.

PR flights by the 13th Squadron commenced from Mount Farm on 28 March 1943 with the 14th joining in during July. The squadrons became part of the 7th Photograph Group on 7 July 1943. Activated on 1 May 1943, the 7th Photograph Group almost at once became the 7th PR and Mapping Group until redesignated on 13 November 1943, the 7th Photograph Group (Reconnaissance). A fourth squadron, No 27, joined the Group on 4 November 1943, and commenced operations on 30 December 1943. It, too, used P-38s, F-4s and F-5s. The first PR sortie to Berlin by a Spitfire from Mount Farm was flown on 6 March. Maps for ground forces and air forces were produced by the group which observed enemy transport movements, installations and gathered weather information. L-5s were used for close support work. In the run-up to D-Day airfields, towns, French ports, targets in the Low Countries were all watched by the 7th.

During July 1944, attention was diverted to V-1 sites and, in August 1944, to gathering information for up-dated maps for the fast advancing army. Photographs were also provided for September's airborne assault and, in December 1944, for the Battle of the Bulge. In the last months of the war, P-51s assigned to the Group escorted its reconnaissance aircraft. On 9 November 1944, 27 Squadron left for France and later Chalgrove. The other three squadrons disbanded during December 1945 after flying post-war damage assessment flights.

The headquarters of the 7th moved to Chalgrove on 8 April 1945, soon followed by the three squadrons. Mount Farm returned to RAF on 1 May 1945, becoming Benson's satellite again from 22 June 1945 to 19 October 1946. No 8 OTU was here until 4 July 1946 when it moved to Chalgrove. Mount Farm became a depot for surplus military vehicles. It was being used for farming by 1949 and was finally sold in 1957. A gravel excavation site marks the position of the airfield.

Shellingford

SU325940. 4 miles E of Faringdon, by A417

Many wartime Elementary Flying Training Schools originated in pre-war organizations. No 3 EFTS, Shellingford's wartime user, began as the Reserve Flying School, Hamble, which opened on 1 April 1931. It became 3 E&RFTS, equipped mainly with Hart variants.

In 1940 flying training around Southampton Water was hazardous and in July the unit's unusual, civilian marked Avro Cadets flew to Watchfield. There, 3 EFTS ran into more problems. Mixing blind approach training with elementary pilot training was hardly ideal.

The search for a practice landing ground to relieve Watchfield commenced. Kelmscot, available for Brize Norton, small and irregularly used, was proposed, but 50 Group showed little inclination to settle for it. In August 1940, 3 EFTS managed 1,935.40 flying hours, and had only two accidents. The search for a landing ground continued and the choice fell, in October, upon a small area near Shellingford, four miles east of Faringdon. Judged to be a good site, surface preparation was needed whilst its main attraction lay in the ease of possible enlargement.

December 1940 brought proposals from Flying Training Command that 3

EFTS take over Wanborough RLG, dormant and awaiting use by Lyneham's SFTS. Wanborough, claimed 3 EFTS, was unsuitable because its grass surface could not accept winter activity. due to increased flying at Watchfield, 3 EFTS decided, in May 1941, to accept Wanborough. Command's response was that the site was now earmarked for Lyneham, and 3 EFTS was authorized to use Kelmscot for practice forced landings. No Tiger Moths were based there for the site was unguarded. At night it was obstructed by an odd collection of vehicles placed there by a local farmer on behalf of Air Ministry.

Closure of 11 Air Observer and Navigator School at Watchfield during July 1941 brought suggestions that 3 EFTS stay there. Since early 1941 3 EFTS's choice of an area near Shellingford had interested higher echelons, and planning was going ahead to acquire it. Orders were received by 3 EFTS on 6 September 1941 that, because upgrading of Kelmscot was unlikely, and because a third Flight was added to the EFTS, a move must come. The new C Flight would be detached to Shellingford until that airfield won full station status.

Shellingford was soon fit for use, obstructions littering it being removed. At a dispersal site pupils had dormitory accommodation from which they were conveyed by motor coach. As yet there were no cooking facilities, meals for the defence force permanently stationed there being brought from Watchfield. Tiger Moths of C Flight dispersed on the airfield, but inspections were carried out at Watchfield.

September 1941 brought instructions from 50 Group that EFTS pupils should have night flying experience to relieve pressure on SFTSs. It commenced at Watchfield on 25 September 1941, only for instructors. Pupils began night flying at Shellingford on 15 October 1941. A Cranwell-type flare path proved satisfactory, and 3 EFTS night training was undertaken there.

On 18 December 1941, with suffcent buildings erected, 3 EFTS moved its 56 Tiger Moths to Shellingford. The technical site had four hangars along with stores, lecture rooms, a Link Trainer, transport section, armoury, flight offices, crew room, parachute section, administration block, nine Nissen huts, three Laing huts for the defence force and a collection of 'latrines — bucket seat type'. A communal site was established at Stanford in the Vale, where the Officers', Sergeants' and Airmens' Messes were, along with the NAAFI, and central ablutions. Officers' and Sergeants' quarters

A daily sight over Shellingford, and many a grass surfaced RLG, a de Havilland Tiger Moth whose pilot is completing a solo flight.

were at dispersed Site 1, each with three sets of huts. Other sites were soon in use and sick quarters was placed at No 5.

In January the use of RLG Kingston Bagpuize was authorized. By mid-January 1942 enough accommodation was available for thirty cadets, and 3 EFTS started to use it as an RLG. Kingston Bagpuize was only briefly available to 3 EFTS so, on 16 May 1942, a detachment went to RLG Wanborough, no longer needed by Lyneham which was making itself a base for heavy transports. Wanborough, though, was too far away from 3 EFTS to be of much value.

Army pilots first joined 3 EFTS in July 1942, for pre-glider flying training. They had to complete eighty hours' dual and solo flying before posting to a GTS. Glider pilot courses were an important part of Shellingford's activity into 1943. Some measure of activity at 3 EFTS may be judged from the 3,472.45 hours flown in March 1943, 209.05 of them at night.

A steady flow of trainees passed through 3 EFTS in 1943 and Tiger Moths were a common sight here. Training of army pilots continued spasmodically and, in September 1945, a period of glider pilot refresher training took place.

Shellingford resumed its association with Watchfield after the war, messing being switched to the latter station. In 1946, Royal Netherlands Air Force pilots trained at Shellingford. With the gradual wind down of the RAF, 3 EFTS, like Shellingford, closed on 31 March 1948.

Stanton Harcourt

SP415050 SW of Stanton Harcourt village. 3½ miles S of A40 at Eynsham.
Late in the afternoon of 6 August 1940, when civilian workmen were busy on one of Stanton Harcourt's hard runways, three enemy bombers suddenly swooped, strafing and bombing. Five of the Wimpey work force were killed and later another four died of their wounds. As a result Anti-Aircraft defences were installed at developing airfields.

Work on Stanton Harcourt, little damaged in the raid, was hastened. On 3 September 1940, No 10 OTU, whose

satellite Stanton Harcourt became, commenced night flying here. Until 15 January 1946, when Stanton Harcourt closed, it reflected 10 OTU's activities. Whitleys of C Flight moved here from Abingdon on 10 September 1940, concentrating on night flying training. Shortage of aircraft caused the Flight to disband in February 1941, then A Flight, converting crews to Whitley flying, replaced it.

Stanton Harcourt had an unusual layout in that its three runways were placed far apart. The proximity of the river Windrush made flooding ever a possibility. Weapons were stored in the southeast of the airfield, main dispersals being on eastern and western sides. Personnel were accommodated in dispersal sites north of the village beyond the 'T2' and 'B1' hangars. Most buildings were of 1940 and 1941 vintage. The runways were put to good use in July 1941 when Halifaxes of 35 and 76 Squadrons attacked the *Scharnhorst*, in La Pallice, from Stanton.

Whitley V operational trainers provided most of the air activity throughout 1942. However, 12 January 1943 brought a most auspicious event. In great secrecy Group Captain van der Kloot flew the famous Liberator, *AL504, Commando*, from Lyneham for Operation *Static*. Early on 13 January *Commando* left, carrying Sir Winston Churchill to the Casablanca Conference.

Reorganization of 10 OTU came in February 1943. A and B Conversion Flights were positioned at Stanton Harcourt and gunnery trainers joined them. From 18 April 1943 until 31 December 1943, Oxfords of 1501 BAT Flight, were here and a 'B1' hangar was erected. On 20 March 1944, 10 OTU's flying was switched to Stanton Harcourt while two runways were laid at Abingdon, and was reduced to ¾ OTU strength in May. Soon after, Hurricanes replaced the fighter-affiliation Martinets. Wellington Xs began to replace Whitley Vs in July, 10 OTU bidding farewell to its last Whitley Vs in October 1944. On 16 November 1944, daylight flying was resumed at Abingdon and most of the unit moved there by early 1945. Stanton Harcourt retired from

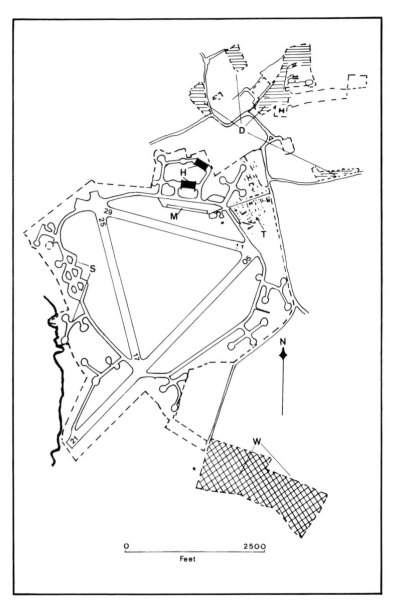

Stanton Harcourt was modified in 1943, hence the loop heavy bomber hardstandings marked **S**. *An unusual feature was the metal planked area nearest to the 'T2' hangar* **M**. *The other hangar was a 'B1', both hangars are marked* **H**. **T** *Technical and administrative site* **D** *Domestic sites, the central one contains communal features* **W** *Weapons storage area. Note the proximity of the River Windrush on the western side.*

active use in the summer of 1945. Parts of the airfield have become busily worked gravel pits.

Upper Heyford

SP515260. 5 miles NW of Bicester, near A43(T)

Upper Heyford was laid down in 1916. A year later Canadians arrived for the formation, on 20 January 1918 of No 123 Squadron, which equipped itself with Sopwith Dolphins before changing its name to No 2 Squadron, Canadian Air Force, early in 1919. Then it left for Shoreham. A second such squadron, also Dolphin equipped, was No 81, formed on 20 November 1918 and later known as No 1 Squadron, Canadian Air Force. This moved to Shoreham in March 1919. First World War Upper Heyford closed in 1920.

Selection of the First World War airfield site for development followed the 1924 Defence Review. Although incomplete, Heyford reopened as a bomber station,

on 12 October 1927. Station Headquarters formed on 25 October and also the Oxford University Flight which acquired three Avro 504Ns. It was renamed Upper Heyford Station Flight on 4 November 1927.

From Bircham Newton, on 12 December 1927, came the advance party of 99 (Bomber) Squadron to prepare Upper Heyford to receive a dozen Hyderabads on 5 January 1928. For company they had 10 Squadron, reformed two days previously. Upper Heyford was starting its long career as a bomber station where, on 25 January 1928, 10 Squadron took on charge its first three Hyderabads. Equipping was a long drawn out process, the usual plea of money shortage abounding. Not until 15 October 1928 did its second Flight form, also with Hyderabads, but on 26 April 1930 the squadron still had only six aircraft.

During 1929 the first Hinaidis reached 99 Squadron. Apart from their Bristol Jupiter engines they differed little from the Hyderabads. During 1930 the squad-

Upper Heyford was home for such aircraft as the 'all string and struts' Handley Page Hyderabads of 99 Squadron.

An ideal model subject and a splendid item for an Upper Heyford open day, Hyderabad J9293 of 99 Squadron. Cor!

ron began to receive later metal Hinaidis. Production remained pathetically slow and into 1931 Hyderabads were still with 99 Squadron. The first Hinaidi for 10 Squadron reached Upper Heyford on 9 December 1930 and by April 1931 it held five. A change in emphasis came when, after its formation on 1 April, 40 Squadron — the first to have Fairey Gordons — led to 10 Squadron moving to Boscombe Down.

No 18 Squadron was resurrected on 20 October 1931 and supplied with Hawker Harts. Its two other Flights,

Below Harts of 18 Squadron two of the Type 'A' Aircraft Sheds may just be glimpsed, still in use at a vastly extended and modified Upper Heyford.

formed on 31 March 1932, were joined by Harts of 57 Squadron on 5 September 1932. Both squadrons became the core of the station's bomber force to the outbreak of war. Abingdon's availability brought space to Upper Heyford for 40 Squadron which was repositioned there in October 1932.

Although re-equipment was long overdue, 99 Squadron soldiered on with its antiques until 14 November 1933 when it took on charge the RAF's first two Handley Page Heyfords. In sombre green, the Heyford had a distinctive shape, and clambering aboard was a memorable experience. Curious indeed seemed the attachment of the fuselage to the underside of the upper mainplane, causing fuselage entry to be made by means of a steep, narrow ladder leading from the lower mainplane on to which one had first to scramble. The peculiar arrangement allowed a dustbin turret to be fitted under the narrow cross section fuselage. Strange, too, were the very narrow tyres set within huge spats. After a crawl along the fuselage one emerged into an open cockpit high above the ground in this 'poor man's Stirling'. A few wriggles more and one was situated in

splendid isolation in the nose gunner's position, albeit being able to turn for company to the pilot close behind. A year to the day from receipt of its first Heyfords, 99 Squadron commenced moving to Mildenhall. That move made space for Harts of 33 Squadron from nearby Bicester. A year later they hurried to Egypt, answering the Italian attack on Abyssinia.

Harts of 18 Squadron temporarily vacated Upper Heyford in January 1936 and were replaced by two lodger squadrons of Vickers Virginias nudged out of Worthy Down, Nos 58 and 215, awaiting Driffield's opening in September 1936. No 18 Squadron then returned, Hind equipped. Bomber Command had then formed and Upper Heyford was in No 1 (Bomber) Group.

New Squadrons came from Flights of existing formations, 218 Squadron from 57 Squadron on 16 March 1936, the parent squadron re-equipping with Hinds in May. Then, 57 Squadron surrendered its B Flight on 4 January 1937 to become 108 Squadron which left for Farnborough the following month. B Flight of 57 Squadron then changed into being 226 Squadron which moved to Harwell in April 1937.

One of the few RAF aircraft types to be named after an aerodrome was the Handley Page Heyford with which 99 Squadron equipped during its stay at Upper Heyford.

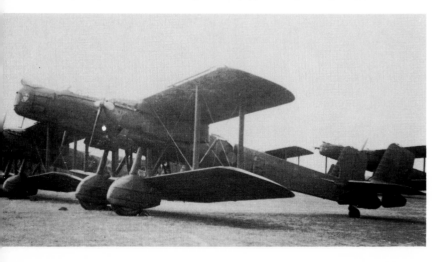

Virginias often floated around over the Midlands, the 58 Squadron example shown being a visitor to Heyford.

Another Hind squadron, formed here on 18 May 1937, was No 113 which went to Grantham in August.

An event which received wide publicity was the formation here in January 1938 of the Long Range Development Flight. Five much-modified Wellesleys, able to carry 1,290 gallons of fuel for their special Pegasus engines, joined the LRDF commanded by Wing Commander O. R. Gayford of Fairey Long-Range Monoplane fame. A 32 hour flight was made in July 1938 from Cranwell to the Persian Gulf. In November, two aircraft made a

18 Squadron later used Hawker Hinds, among them K5471 which served between April 1936 and June 1939.

Above *Wellesleys of the Long Range Development Unit.*

Above left *Harts of 57 Squadron airborne from Upper Heyford.*

Left *Hind K5426 of 40 Squadron releases a practice bomb.*

Below *In February 1938 218 Squadron equipped with Fairey Battles, and moved to Boscombe Down the following April taking K7666 among others.*

Blenheim 1 L1145 of 57 Squadron, beside one of Upper Heyford's hangars.

spectacular record flight from Egypt to Australia non-stop in 48 hours, unbeaten for eight years.

Upper Heyford's bomber squadrons were ever changing. Hinds of 218 Squadron left in April 1938, making way for the monoplane era. It began with Bristol Blenheim 1s and soon the station became one of their most prominent bases as 57 Squadron rapidly worked up with the wonder-bomber in March–April 1938 with 34 Squadron joining the sport in July. That had vacated Lympne and left behind its Hinds.

In May 1938, 18 Squadron received Blenheims, the three squadrons during the Munich Crisis awaiting to become part of the 2nd Echelon, AASF, France before the crisis passed. January 1939 found Upper Heyford placed in 2 Group which, in February, shifted 34 Squadron to newly opened Watton. Upper Heyford faced the coming storm with some stability, the base for two front-line Blenheim 1 squadrons. Their role within 70 Wing, Air Component, BEF, was to provide aerial reconnaissance for the British Army in France.

At the commencement of hostilities, Upper Heyford and its satellite field at Brackley (later known as Croughton) were immediately placed in No 6 Group and into a training role. Both Blenheim

squadrons left for France as planned, 18 Squadron going to Amy and 57 to Roye, both on 24 September 1939.

On the day previous to that move, SHQ Finningley arrived, bringing two Hampden squadrons, Nos 7 and 76, to become 5 Group Pool. No 76 was half Hampden equipped, its other Flight using Anson navigation trainers. This training establishment ran until 22 April 1940 when SHQ closed and 5 Group Pool became 16 OTU within 6 Group. Steady expansion followed and, on 7 May 1940, the OTU received the first of nineteen troublesome Handley Page Herefords. A month later more Ansons arrived. Training took a steady toll of lives, 13 August 1940 bringing a spectacular midday crash. Two Hampdens, *L4138* and *P4339*, barely airborne, collided in a gruesome smash when taking off from different grass runways.

On 25 and 27 July 1940, handfuls of Hampdens set off on leaflet dropping sorties, carrying out the station's first offensive action. An operations order of 8 August called for up to eight such sorties weekly, in response to which Hampdens of 16 OTU visited Caen, Rennes and Brest. Croughton landing ground began to be much used in July, accommodation being at Rastwick and Rectory Farms for ground crew controlling the busy night

Throughout the war Avro Ansons were a daily Oxfordian sight. The example shown is believed to have been at Upper Heyford before the war.

flying procedures and equipment. More leaflet drops took place in October, then operations stopped.

Throughout 1941, Upper Heyford housed 16 OTU, training up to 24 one-pilot crews for Hampdens each month. The OTU was using widely spread accommodation, in Aynho Park, Fritwell Manor, Fucott House, Middleton, sundry stone cottages and in Nissen huts which decorated the area around the station.

In April 1941, due to their poor serviceability record, the Herefords were posted away, to 5 B&GS. The established strength at that time was 49 Hampden/ Herefords, thirteen Ansons, twelve Oxfords and sundry light aircraft.

Barford St John replaced Croughton as satellite in 1942, use also being made of Hinton-in-the-Hedges. Another advance came in April 1942 for by the end of that month, 16 OTU had received 23 Wellington 1cs. Only the course underway flew Hampdens. The first Wellington joined the OTU on 25 April, the first crew output being made on 5 June 1942.

May 1942 found 16 OTU half equipped with Wellingtons, sufficiently so for fourteen of them and sixteen Hampdens to take part in the Cologne 1,000 bomber raid from here. For the Essen attack of

1-2 June, thirty crews operated, again in a mixed force. Hampden *P2080* was attacked by a German fighter, in exchange for which the crew claimed to shoot down another. Twenty-three crews operated Wellington 1cs in June's Bremen 1,000 bomber operation. More bombing raids were flown in July, August and September.

By March 1943, the OTU's strength had risen to 57 Wellington 1cs, six Ansons, a Defiant and two Lysander target towers. Alongside, enveloped in great secrecy, was 1473 Flight whose origin lay within the RCM Flight of 109 Squadron. That formation broke away on 10 July 1942 from the organization which achieved fame as a result of its so-called 'beam bending' activities in 1940. It was now an independent unit under Flight Lieutenant C. F. Grant, DFC, controlled by 80 Wing and administered by 92 Group. Using Ansons and Wellingtons, it monitored German radio beam activity whilst participating in *Window* trials for Bomber Command before moving to Finmere in 1943. No 1505 BAT Flight's Oxfords, also within 92 Group, provided beam approach practice from Upper Heyford between 17 December 1942 and its disbandment on 20 February 1943. Wellington IIIs came into use at 16

OTU in September 1942, their improved performance causing 92 Group to issue an order in November that four *Nickelling* sorties be flown per fortnight. From Upper Heyford leaflet dropping was resumed on 27-28 November with drops in the Nantes area. In between *Bullseyes*, propaganda leaflets were dropped on Paris on 20-21 December 1942.

Such activities continued throughout 1943, in the autumn of which Wellington Xs joined the OTU in increasing proportion. In 1944, too, the pattern of activity was all but the same. At the end of December, No 1655 Mosquito Training Unit arrived with an assortment of Mosquito bombers and trainers along with a selection of Oxfords. The old 16 OTU disbanded, its title at once being conferred upon the new arrival which also used Barford St John. For training, bomber crews for 8 Group 16 OTU's nominal strength in March 1945 stood at 45 Mosquitoes of Mks 3, 4, 6, 20 and 25

supported, for navigation and light bombing training, by as many as 32 Oxfords, all under 92 Group control and shared in positioning with Barford. Immediate postwar days witnessed a reduction in strength before 16 OTU moved to Cottesmore in March 1946. In its place came Dakotas of the Parachute Training School. Also brought here was the famous parachute training tower which came from Ringway and moved to Abingdon in 1950.

The reason for that move was that the Americans were coming in June 1950. They took over four barrack blocks and the Airmens' Mess, using facilities for a US Engineer Aviation Battalion, a Maintenance Company, Ordnance Company, Engineer Depot Company and the Base Support Company. These units, which soon increased in strength had come to support the expanding SAC force moving into East Anglia and the Midlands. Barford St John remained Upper Heyford's

satellite, like Middleton Stoney. Weston-on-the-Green which, since 1946, had been under Upper Heyford's control became the home of the Air Position Plotting Unit on 9 August 1950 and, at the end of April 1951, was transferred to No 62 (Signals) Group, RAF. On 15 May 1951, control of Upper Heyford passed to the USAF, formal handover from 3 (Bomber) Group being staged on 1 June when the 7509th Air Base Squadron took control.

Upper Heyford's main runway was some 6,000 ft long and 150 ft wide, the Americans' first task being to lengthen it to some 10,000 ft. By the end of 1951, with the 7509th ready to support operational units, the first TDY element arrived, the 93rd Air Refuelling Squadron flying Boeing KB-29Ps from Castle AFB at the start of December 1951 for a 90 day stay.

On 10 January 1952 the 3918th Air Base Group took over the running of the base where the RAFs PTS held lodger unit status.

American construction of specialized facilities for use by SAC included three nose docks for large aircraft and a new maintenance building. Among the units based at Upper Heyford in 1952 was the 98th Smoke Generating Company, there to provide a smoke screen in the event of air attack. Further afield defence was soon provided by light Anti-Aircraft guns of the 4th AA Artillery Battalion. By then Upper Heyford had hosted KB-29P aerial refuellers of the 97th, 509th and 2nd BGs as well as KB-29Ms whose role was in-flight refuelling of B-29s of the 301st BG. Sundry sections of KB-29s and B-50Ds were temporarily stationed at Upper Heyford before, in June 1953, the first B-47B

Boeing B-29s, KB-29s and B-50s all made use of Upper Heyford in the 1950s. 8052 was a standard B-50D. (Boeing.)

During its detachment to England in spring 1955, this B-47E-35-35-LM of the 310th Bomb Wing (M) was based at Upper Heyford.

Stratojets in Britain began using the base. Thenceforth many B-47s and RB-47s lodged here. On 5 February 1954, a B-47 was involved in a spectacular crash in Stoke Wood, 1½ miles from the end of the main runway. Not long after, some of the first B-47Es in Britain were based here.

Mid-1954 witnessed the first landings at Upper Heyford of RB-36H reconnaissance aircraft of the 5th SRW whose main base was Fairford. Principally, nuclear-armed Stratojets made Upper Heyford their home — until 31 March 1965 when the SAC mission ended and the base was transferred to United States Air Force (Europe). Upper Heyford then came under the care of the 7514th Combat Support Group who maintained it as a Dispersed Operating Base (DOB). That status terminated on 1 September 1966 with the arrival of the 66th Tactical Reconnaissance Wing from Laon,

KC-97 tanker aircraft were also often sited here during their three month temporary duty stays in Britain. Although stationed at Brize Norton in May 1955, this KC-97F-75-BO of the 310th Air Refuelling Squadron also flew from Upper Heyford.

Assorted RB-47 electronic intelligence gatherers of the 55th SRW were often tucked well away from public view while on detachment to Upper Heyford.

France. The 7514th was de-activated and Heyford became a Main Operating Base housing RF-101C Voodoos until their unit was de-activated on 1 April 1970, a year after RF-4Cs had been placed in the 17th Tactical Reconnaissance Squadron.

Their place was taken by the present residents, F-111Es of the 20th Tactical Fighter Wing. The new assignment meant a change of mission for the 20th and extensive modifications to the base, resulting in the station being the largest of its kind in Europe. On 12 September 1970, the first two F-111E swing wing bombers touched down at Upper Heyford, the 20th having its full complement by 29 July 1971. By September 1980 the F-111Es had flown over 55,000 training sorties.

The F-111Es of the 20th TFWs 55th (blue), 77th (red) and 79th (yellow) Squadrons were joined late 1983 by the 42nd Electronic Combat Squadron

RF-101C Voodoos were at Upper Heyford at the time when camouflage began to become general on USAF UK-based aircraft, as on 60079.

Above Since September 1970 F-111Es like 68-036 have been resident at Upper Heyford. Initially they wore the tail identity 'JR'. Well he has replaced 'Uncle Sam' hasn't he?

Above right One of the most unusual sights at UK USAF bases in the late 1960s and early 1970s was the Kaman HH-43B twin rotor rescue and fire fighting helicopter. 24536 was one of a pair based at Upper Heyford.

Below right EF-111A Raven 041/UH electronic counter measures aircraft based at Upper Heyford. Three operated during Operation Eldorado Canyon, the USAF strike on Libya in 1986.

Below Before adopting toned down markings the F-111Es changed their tail letters to UH, as on the often displayed 68-077.

assigned to the 20th, and which became equipped with pale grey-camouflaged EF-111A Raven electronic warfare aircraft. On 1 July 1985 the 66th Electronic Combat Wing formed at Sembach, Germany, to which the 42nd ECS was assigned. Five Ravens took part in Operation *Eldorado Canyon* on 14–15 April 1986, the American attack on Tripoli's terrorist targets. Two of the EF-111s were back-up to the three neutralizing Libyan radar.

It is hard to believe, but F-111s have served longer in Oxfordshire than any other type of operational aircraft.

Watchfield

SU240900. 6 miles N of Swindon, by A420

Watchfield's contribution to the winning of the war is impossible to assess, but it certainly played an important part in improving the safe return of many an operational crew. The availability of the station in July 1940 brought along Tiger Moths of 3 EFTS, a unit formed at Hamble on 1 January 1940 from the pre-war 3 E&RFTS and forced out of its siting by Southampton Water when the Battle of Britain opened. At Watchfield the School

arrived on 20 July 1940 as Ansons of 4 AONS were arriving from Ansty and others of 11 AONS were fleeing from Hamble. Watchfield was over-populated, yet more occupants would follow. The intention was for No 1 Blind Approach School to form here on 2 August 1940 but lack of suitable equipment delayed this. Instead, the School commenced activity here on 28 October 1940 and was operated by Air Service Training, a subsidiary of Hawker Siddeley. Four Ansons, with two in reserve, were placed at the unit, along with three wheel-type link trainers. The task was the training of pilots in blind approach flying techniques, increasingly important as night flying increased.

Blind approach training had commenced at Mildenhall in March 1939, first using Anson L9155 fitted with blind approach receivers (R1124/1125). Commanding the small formation was Squadron Leader R. S. Blucke, AFC. In July 1939 the Anson was alloted to 24 Squadron, Hendon. VHF blind approach equipment was then in full use at Boscombe Down. The precious Anson was taken from Hendon on 1 September 1939 and placed at CFS Upavon, pending the establishment of a blind approach training development unit at Boscombe Down to where the Anson was transferred on 22 September 1939. More Ansons were then fitted with blind approach equipment

and, by May 1940, the 20th short course was underway.

On 6 June 1940, orders were received from 23 Group to close the school, and Wing Commander Blucke was posted to HQ Bomber Command. On 13 June 1940, the unit reopened, but for a totally different purpose. The establishment was raised to eight Ansons and three Whitleys, the new task was to investigate unusual enemy radio signals code name 'Headache'. Operational control was vested in Fighter Command, the unit having five Ansons with suitable equipment. Pilots from the old BATDU were posted to the new unit and included Flight Lieutenant H. E. Bufton who arrived from 214 Squadron to command. Two days later he took Anson N9945 to Wyton to commence radio investigation into the German use of radio beams for navigation purposes and target marking. Such operations were soon busily engaged upon.

By October the unit's role had so far altered that, on the 14th, its name changed from Blind Approach Training and Development Unit to Wireless Intelligence Development Unit, a title which had been in colloquial use since 30 September 1940. Meanwhile the need ever increased for specialized blind approach training. No longer could formation of a specialized unit answering

The welcoming entrance to RAF Watchfield. (Squadron Leader G. M. Phillips, MBE.)

needs be overlooked. On 20 October 1940, Watchfield received two Ansons from the WIDU, *R9828* and *R9830*, both carrying beam approach equipment. On the following day, *R9829* and *R9837* joined them and initial equipment was complete for a Blind Approach School. If an element of secrecy was needed it was easy to achieve since navigation training Ansons were busy in the circuit.

Ground equipment for blind approach training was in short supply. Main beacon, as well as the inner and outer marker beacons, were of a type made by Philips in Holland and no longer obtainable and more advanced than the British standard type. Its main beacon had a system of phased aerials which reduced the twilight zone. Only at Schiphol Airport in the Netherlands had such advanced equipment been installed and Watchfield's had been shipped to Britain before the Netherlands fell. All the Ansons now at Watchfield had receivers working with this system, already used at Boscombe Down.

Six pupils arrived on 28 October 1940 at the commencement of the first of the first two-week course. That involved twelve hours' flying to a schedule laid down by Wing Commander R. S. Blucke. Training commenced with time on the Link Trainer, during which trainees listened to beam approach notes in headphones and had the figure-of-eight flying procedures demonstrated.

From the start it was obvious that there would be considerable flying training problems at this busy station. Tiger Moths of the EFTS were ever active on circuit and Ansons setting off on longer flights. Control of the flying, from the tower, was vested in an instructor of the Blind Approach School who saw to it that when an aircraft was on blind approach a red light on the tower was switched 'on'. This indicated to EFTS pilots that the incoming aircraft was at 100 ft in the direction of the main beam, irrespective of the wind direction. All aircraft on the ground had to remain stationary when the red light was 'on'.

During the winter, training proceeded satisfactorily, despite a visit by the enemy on the evening of 27 February 1941. Incendiaries fell, along with a stick of five HEs along the south-east boundary of the airfield. Even less successful in display was the blind approach equipment when the Inspector General, Air Marshal Sir W. Mitchell, arrived in his Cygnet on 19 May 1941. As he was about to watch the demonstration a resistance burnt out in the main beacon, putting everything out of use!

By mid-1941, installation of blind approach equipment had been extended to units in other parts of Britain. Reliability of the equipment and its accurate calibration needed to be regularly checked so, in May 1941, the Blind Approach Calibration Flight formed at Watchfield, equipped with three Oxfords, the first aircraft of that type to be used for any blind approach duties. Over the next month, three more — *V3888, V4026* and *V4027* — arrived. Any slight increase in flying at Watchfield brought problems, so it is hardly surprising that No 11 AONS closed on 19 July 1941 and No 4 on 30 August 1941.

Mid-August saw discussions into the means of considerably increasing the output of trainees. Existing flying programmes called for eighteen hours' flying each day, 24 hours being deemed impossible to maintain because. of enemy activity, unserviceability, etc. A scheme to train 1,100 pilots a year was to be put in hand, which meant an increase in aircraft establishment from six to fifteen and of instructors from seven to sixteen. On 1 September 1941, as an interim measure, the establishment changed to twelve Ansons, an event soon overtaken. Blind approach training would now be part of the training syllabus at SFTSs, where the standard aircraft type was the Airspeed Oxford. To achieve standardization it was decided to re-equip No 1 Blind Approach School with Oxfords, a decision made on 16 September 1941 to help dispel a generally held and erroneous notion that blind approach training could only be effectively carried out using Ansons because Oxfords were less well mannered. On the following day, three more Oxfords,

V4051, *V4052* and *V5054* arrived at Watchfield.

Another alteration became effective at Watchfield on 26 September 1941 when night flying throughout the hours of darkness commenced. It depended upon a Cranwell type flarepath, power for which was supplied from the floodlight beacon. Flying took place every night so that new training programme demands might be met, for the rate of trainee arrivals was now twelve every four days for a twelve day course. In the twelve months ending 28 October 1941, 405 pupils were trained, sixty per cent for night fighter duties. An enviable flight safety record had been achieved for there had been merely one forced landing brought about when a pupil knocked off some switches upon changing seats. No other accident had marred the School's record. Additionally, pilots of the School had, since 13 March 1941, been training wireless mechanics. Introduction of the 24 hour flying scheme, on 8 September 1941, improved the pupil output rate. In October 1941 the unit was redesignated No 1 Beam Approach School.

From Brasenose College, Oxford, the Regional Control School of Bomber Command moved into Watchfield on 15 December 1941, becoming the School of Flying Control. Lecture rooms for the School were available after the departure of 3 EFTS to Shellingford on 18 December 1941. Trials of the Bell and Bobbitt trailing wire device, intended to inform the pilot accurately of his height, were conducted in January 1942.

Watchfield's first serious flying accident occurred on 2 February, involving *AT775*, flown by Sergeant C. M. Rustron. January had ended with snow and very cold weather which extended into February. As this Oxford was approaching, ice accretion on the wings seriously increased and snow obliterated the pupil's vision, forcing him to make a very difficult blind landing. A stall developed, the port wing dropped and the aircraft side-slipped in from about 15 ft.

Four Dominies were allocated to BAS on 9 February 1942 to give SFC pupils air experience. On the following day the first attempt to locate a suitable airfield site for blind approach training was undertaken. Firstly a landing ground at Bushy Barn, Pusey, near Burford was inspected, but it was quite unsuitable.

By mid-March 1942 another Flight was needed in order to train 1,450 pilots a year from April. Trials on 22 April 1942 proved it was possible for an Oxford to be landed every five minutes as a revised holding pattern was introduced. By that time three Dominies — *X7491*, *X7492* and *X7493* — had arrived and, in May, Oxfords from Docking's BAT Flight were posted in to equip the new, additional Flight. To simulate night flying in daylight, synthetic night flying was tried using Oxford *V4051*. On 16 May 1942, the aircraft was flying with blue window panels, its pilot wearing special goggles.

The association with the SFC had, by July 1942, brought along a new RAF trade, airfield controller. Things moved fast, the first trainees arriving on 18 July 1942, comprising 34 ORs here for a two-week course. A few days previously, Oxfords of the Calibration Flight moved to Bicester, easing some of the pressure on Watchfield. By November, use of existing beam approach equipment at nearby stations was being made. Those at Boscombe Down, Abingdon, Harwell and Little Rissington were used, and equipment at Watchfield's new satellite, Kelmscot, came into use on 17 October 1942. Each course now lasted a week because the other beams were available.

Sudden changes in weather posed major problems in this busy area, as when general weather deterioration came quickly on 6 January 1943. One pupil landed safely at Kelmscot meaning that an overnight guard had to be placed on the aircraft. Flying Officer Hutchison, flying *V4049*, was over Otmoor when ordered back to base. His homing equipment failed and when he eventually arrived over Watchfield he discovered that the undercarriage would not lock in the 'down' position, so that aircraft had to be abandoned.

Flying was drastically reduced for a period of six weeks early in 1943 while contact lighting was installed, and at a time when the airfield surface was very wet and the laying of a flare path impracticable. Some flying was possible at RLG Kelmscot.

Operational aircraft as well as others were kept well away from busy Watchfield, except in emergencies. One such came on the night of 10 June 1943 when, at 01:43, the Duty Flying Controller heard a large, low-flying aircraft. There was soon an explosion, and flames poured from the wreckage, a mile north-west of the airfield. They marked where a Lancaster from Lindholme crashed, killing the crew of seven.

By July 1943, the second RLG, Wanborough, was in regular use, mainly for training airfield controllers. Up to 110 pupils at a time trained there, each course spending half its training period at this RLG. Kelmscot RLG was busily in use whilst a few personnel manned Watchfield's Q-site at Kingston Warren.

It was Flight Lieutenant James in Oxford 'H' who, at 17:25 on 22 October 1943, gave the station warning of startling, impending disaster. Using his R/T he reported something akin to a whirlwind approaching the airfield from the south. Moments later it was possible to see from the tower a mass of *nimbo stratus* coming from the direction of Shrivenham, and with a dark funnel hanging from it. Two Oxfords about to take off were ordered to taxi quickly back to the tower. The violent disturbance passed across the airfield towards the NNE, snatching a metal sheet off a hangar and depositing it in the middle of the landing ground. Oxford 'S' was lifted 10 ft into the air, swung around then dropped. Its undercarriage collapsed and the port wing crumpled. Two others were damaged before the intense storm died suddenly away.

At the end of 1943, the Beam Approach Technical Training School moved to No 1 Radio School, Cranwell. On 18 December 1943, the training of airfield controllers was transferred from Wanborough to Watchfield and Kelmscot, allowing 3 GTS to place on Flight at Wanborough because Stoke Orchard was temporarily out of use. Wanborough

Watchfield's unusual control tower. (Squadron Leader G. M. Phillips, MBE.)

was vacated by the School of Airfield Controllers on 2 December 1944 due to the poor state of personnel accommodation there, although the School still made some use of it.

By March 1944 the area around Watchfield was highly congested by the influx of transport aircraft — and worse, by gliders taking part in ever increasingly large exercises. With flying control becoming ever more important, a master flying control for the whole area was set up at South Cerney. Although Kelmscot was to remain the RLG for Watchfield into 1947, during 1944 it was used a number of times for parachute troop training exercises on a grand scale. Not until after D-Day was the BAS able to use the RLG.

A new BAT syllabus was introduced on 30 August 1944. Full cross-country flying in cloud was now to be practised at (P) AFUs by pilots undergoing BA training. During 1944 the course undertaken by a pilot at No 1 BAS consisted of three unhooded introductory exercises: i) familiarization and orientation, ii) a figure-of-eight flown at constant height and iii) normal approach procedure. During this 'hooded' training he again flew the 'eight' at constant height, the normal and back beam approach, visual and oral signal approaches, QDM homing procedures, homing without QDM, cross country and, finally, engaged in night flying. In addition to 1 BAS, several beam approach and radio aids training flights used Watchfield: 1500 in 1943: 1547, which formed on 1 June 1945 and was here into 1946; and 1557, also formed 1 June 1945 with double the normal eight Oxfords of these Flights, and quickly transferred to 6 (P) AFU.

No 1 BAS disbanded on 1 January 1947, having latterly used a few Harvards as well as Oxfords. In its final months it trained pilots with the aid of two beams operated at Watchfield and Kelmscot, and used other beam systems within a radius of 100 miles. During six years of existence 1 BAS aircraft had flown little short of 100,000 hours, some 8,500 pupils had passed through the School and only one flying accident involving injury had come about during QBI conditions.

An amazing record for sure.

After the war, Watchfield settled to being the centre for the training of airfield control personnel, the School of Air Traffic Control forming the School of Flying Control during April 1946 and remaining until January 1950. In the 1950s new uses were found for Watchfield — parachute training, and as a dropping zone for heavy loads from RAF transports. For these purposes Watchfield has remained in use for many years.

Weston-on-the-Green

SP535205. 3½ miles SW of Bicester by A43(T)

Weston's survivability is amazing, particularly as it never has been much more than a large field. Even more surprising, it has been quite important and must, in several respects, be unique. Additionally, it is one of the few airfields retaining concrete evidence of First World War days albeit little more than foundations.

Apparently the ground was acquired for military use in 1916. By whom it was first used seems now uncertain. Surviving records state that No 28 Training Depot Station opened here on 27 July 1918, arising from an amalgamation of Nos 61 and 70 Training Squadrons. Rotating Clergets of Sopwith Camels therefore rent the peace of the area, along with Avro 504Ks. Ground attack Sopwith Salamanders replaced the Camels before No 28 TDS closed in 1919. Establishment figures suggest that as many as 72 aircraft may have resided here, where six aircraft sheds and a repair shed were provided. Remnants of 18 Squadron came from Germany. No 2 Squadron disbanded here on 20 January 1920, activity ceasing at the site in 1921. Under whose control it was placed remains uncertain, but before the outbreak of war in 1939 it was in the hands of RAF Brize Norton whose satellite it then became. During the intervening years it was grazing land.

On 2 September 1939, upon the order to scatter, No 90 Squadron (and probably 101 Squadron) hurriedly brought its Blenheims to Weston. Next day both squadrons were repositioned at Brize Norton, although some activity connected with both squadrons continued at Weston-on-the-Green until mid-September. Bicester then used Weston for its Ansons and Blenheims. When 13 OTU formed in April 1940 it came under control of that unit, remaining within 7 Group.

Weston-on-the-Green was, on 9 August 1940, the first Oxfordshire airfield to be bombed. Late that night a stick of 16 HEs was released in a 2 mile long line extending from Chesterton to the landing ground upon which five of the bombs exploded without causing damage. A second attack came on 25-26 August when a lot of incendiaries were scattered. The following night the Germans came again, to make seven more holes on Weston's flying field. Persistent Luftwaffe attacks were quite remarkable for on 2-3 September another five HEs fell near Weston and one on Otmoor bombing range. It was almost as if someone was waging a personal war against this small, inoffensive little airfield, instead of the large ones nearby.

In the summer of 1940, 13 OTU obtained more suitable satellites and on 1 November 1940 the station became an RLG for 15 SFTS, Kidlington. Harvards and mainly Oxfords flew daily and often by night. Early in 1941 part of that unit moved to Weston where a detachment of thirty men to service the aircraft now based here, came on 20 February 1941.

Considerable local concern arose when, just after midnight on 12 August 1941, an intruder entered Weston's airspace and joined night flying Oxfords of No 24 Course. After engaging one, the intruder came upon another, opening fire upon it when flying at 4,000 ft. *W6629* promptly burst into flames and both Flight Sergeant Julin-Olsene (Norwegian) and Leading Aircraftsman C. P. Blaire were killed. Wreckage fell near Sturdy's Castle. Then the raider dropped six light bombs on the airfield. Seven Oxfords on the landing ground were damaged by strafing.

The protracted closure of 15 SFTS to clear way for glider training at Kidlington resulted in the contraction of the SFTS

and withdrawal of J and K Flights from Weston on 23 December 1941. By that date No 2 Glider Training School was already functioning at Weston-on-the-Green.

Orders for its formation as an off-shoot of No 1 GTS were received at Thame on 4 December 1941. Over the following few days, Weston's state was examined. It occupied six accommodation sites, in addition to a technical site where about 160 personnel resided. The communal site was 1½ miles away and the dormitory site a further mile from it — such was wartime dispersal for which the bicycle provided the ideal means of transport. A rapid decision was made, a party to open No 2 GTS arriving on 8 December 1941. Airmen and NCOs would be accommodated in huts whilst officers resided comfortably at Kidlington. On 22 December 1941, No 2 GTS was transferred from 70 Group Army Co-operation Command to 23 Group, Training Command.

Shortage of Hotspurs, Hectors tugs and tow ropes was matched by that of flying instructors. Training started early January 1942 after conversion of pilots from Netheravon who had Hawker Hart experience and who would now fly Hawker Hectors. By the end of December 1941, No 2 GTS had eight Hectors, four of which were swopped for two dual control examples at Thame. Another two, without towing hooks, were suitable for pilot training. Maintenance was a problem with these ageing biplanes and their Napier Dagger III engines, further complicated by a shortage of suitable maintenance equipment. Such features ensured an inauspicious start for 2 GTS.

Gliders were slow in coming, the first four arriving as a late Christmas present from 15 MU Wroughton. Assembly, with the help of General Aircraft, commenced on 29 December 1941. This was none too easy for tailplane warping was discovered and two gliders had to be borrowed from Thame to help with initial flying. Nevertheless, a general start had been accomplished and, on 28 December 1941, the first trainees reported to Weston-on-the-Green for flying training,

Weston-on-the-Green in July 1941. Foreground ground markings show the siting of First World War buildings, and there is a motley collection of more modern structures. (PRO.)

where a few Hawker Hinds were now also to hand. Although 15 SFTS had left, one Over Type 'Blister' hangar was set aside for the use of any night flying Oxford which might need servicing during limited use of the aerodrome.

Shortage of tugs for training gliders resulted in a Fairey Battle being tested for the task at Weston in mid-December, and promptly being found unsuitable. In January 1942 winter conditions brought a steady deterioration for the airfield surface which was soon too wet for Hectors. These aircraft performed poorly in winter, whilst the Dagger's characteris-

tics indicated that it would easily overheat in summer during towing activity. This brought about further search for a replacement, resulting in a Kestrel XX engined Hawker Audax, *K5152*. This type, which when towing a Hotspur, needed an 820 yd run to clear 50 ft, was far preferable to the Hector, and Audaxes were acquired as fast as possible for glider towing attachments to be fitted.

January 1942 also witnessed the completion of the twelve bay Bessoneau hangar with another nine bays being constructed. Two more Over Type Blister hangars were being erected, along with

Hawker Hectors towing Hotspur gliders over Oxfordshire. (IWM.)

Above *Hotspur II gliders and Audax tugs at Weston-on-the-Green, summer 1942. Across the field Master II glider tugs are dispersed. Tugs carry large identity numbers, gliders have letters. (IWM.)*

Below *Army personnel (General Browning central) at Weston-on-the-Green on 30 March 1942, standing in front of a Hawker Hector. (Via J. R. Norris.)*

another eight Hotspurs to fill them. Establishment was currently for thirty Hotspurs, twelve plus four (immediate plus reserve) tugs, two Tiger Moths and a Hind (T). The first six week glider pilot's course commenced on 2 January 1942, pass out coming on 17 February. Despite the poor surface, up to six tow lines were then in operation simultaneously, two of these being temporarily made available to 1 GTS whose base at Thame was even more unsuitable for flying than Weston.

Five Audaxes arrived on 7 March and others later that month although they did not entirely replace the Hectors, a few of which remained for full load towing. Two more 'Blister' hangars were erected in April 1942. In March 1942 the projected Hotspur (T) became the Hotspur III and, in April 1942, all Hotspurs were ordered to be completed as training gliders. Some 370 had been built by then and plans were for ten to be much modified to Mk III standard per week. Cost, and ever changing requirements, led to only 52 Mk

III being produced fully modified for glider schools.

Now that the Hotspur II was in service some modifications were very necessary. Tail skids gave trouble and new designs were produced by various agencies, among them Weston's staff. A modification eventually adopted involved backward extension of the foot of the skid which was also made more flexible and able to withstand heavier shocks during landings. There were three more serious accidents in May 1942. One involved a glider which entered a very steep climb just after take off and stalled as the tow rope was released. Then a high point tow developed as another Hotspur took off and had to be released quickly for a forced landing. Trouble with another glider's canopy opening in flight brought further hasty touch-down.

Throughout the month, night flying was also carried out here by Hotspurs of No 102 (Glider) OTU, Kidlington. Search for more suitable landing grounds for glider schools was underway and 2 GTS conducted trials at Long Newton with the idea of its being used for 1 GTS in place of unsuitable Thame. There was also a constant desire to improve the Hotspur's performance. Gliders being built or in preparation depended upon a bifurcated tow rope which meant that extra time was needed in hook-ups. Nose point towing was developed and, by the end of May 1942, Hotspurs were being modified to have the nose towing point, featured by four gliders here by the end of the month.

Using outdated Hawker biplanes to tow the gliders was far from satisfactory. Various replacement aircraft types were again considered for the task, including an Oxford tested here in May before the choice fell upon the Miles Master II. On 16 June the first arrived at Weston for towing equipment. Three dual-control Master IIs arrived on 28 June and conversion training was undertaken with the assistance of instructors from 9 (P) AFU. Two Hotspurs with nose towing points were in regular use.

The Hotspur was far too tail heavy for the Master tug. Ballast had to be carried to ease the problem before research at GTSs and RAE eventually led to a change in the glider's tailplane incidence. By August the glider establishment had doubled and the tug strength set at forty aircraft. On a fine day it was now possible to achieve as many as eighty tows out of Weston. Towing a Hotspur, the Master needed a 900 yd run to reach 50 ft. Standard Manilla tow ropes were 2½ in thick and were suitable for 35 launches.

On 2 September 1942, Master *DL425* was towing *HH518* off from Weston and little height could be gained. Within moments the combination smashed into the steeple of Witney's church. Survival of the occupants was amazing, although their injuries were serious.

Intensive glider pilot training continued into 1943. Conditions at Weston at the start of February were so bad that the unit was detached to Cheddington from where flying took place until 20 March 1943 when return to Weston came. Drastic changes were then underway. Air Ministry Works had, in February, decided

that it was essential that Sommerfeld Tracking runways and peritrack be laid at Weston prior to the next winter. Another decision had been taken to the effect that all glider pilot training at 4 GTS would cease, an order becoming effective on 10 March 1943. The existing 4 GTS became, that same day, retitled 20 (P) AFU. Next, it was the turn of 1 GTS to close, this unit also dissolving into 20 (P) AFU on 24 March 1943. Its Croughton base then became a satellite of Kidlington. Finally came the turn of 2 GTS, Weston, which ceased to function on 6 April 1943 to emerge the very same day, and at Weston, as yet another satellite of 20 (P) AFU. Before that date new occupants arrived and soon three dozen Oxfords were based here. In March, 20 (P) AFU had received 76 Oxfords and three Ansons and later its strength would be double that figure.

Weston had become a satellite of Kidlington and soon came the training accidents which afflicted all such places. On 15 May 1943, Oxford *T1100* crashed into the roof of a cottage on the airfield boundary, an accident from which, luckily, the pilot was extricated.

AMWD were as good as their word and laid Sommerfeld Tracking in September 1943. Thereafter by day — and particularly by night — Oxford flying took place until it was forcibly halted by the disbandment of 20 (P) AFU on 31 May 1945. Weston remained in 23 Group until 1 October 1945 when it came under 3 MU which held it until 15 March 1946. Control then passed to Upper Heyford, a 38 Group station and a part of Transport Command. As soon as 1 PTS reached that station, Weston-on-the-Green began to be used as a dropping zone for parachutists. They were also able to jump from a basket suspended below an LZ Kite Balloon which, for many years, drifted daily above Weston.

The Korean War heralded weeks of high tension to British airfields and Upper Heyford was no exception. On 10 June 1950, Weston was placed at the disposal of Bomber Command which held the station until 9 August 1950 when the Air Positioning Plotting Unit arrived. That was

Paradropping has long been undertaken at Weston, and frequently by Hastings transports like Mk 2 WD494 of 24 Squadron photographed in 1958.

part of 62 Group under whose command Weston remained until 20 April 1951 when the site was placed into a Care and Maintenance state.

With so much transport activity in the area, it was not long before Transport Command repossessed the airfield for use once more as a dropping area for exercises run by 1 PTS. Weston has been used as a DZ for parachutists descending over the years from Valettas, Beverleys, Argosies, Andovers and Hercules. During 1976 the parachutists' captive balloon was removed to Hullavington. Since that time a lot of free fall parachute jumping has taken place, both civil and military, and has included jumps by the RAF Sport Parachute Association.

Weston-on-the-Green houses the Oxford Gliding Club, and the RAFGSA Chiltern Gliding Club which also functions from Bicester. It seems that, come what may, Weston is determined somehow to serve its country.

Witney

SP330095. 1 mile W of Witney, S of the old A40

Witney First World War RFC flying training school was sited on the west side of the town. Training in fighter tactics was undertaken here where, on 30 March 1918, No 8 Training Squadron arrived from Netheravon to be followed by No 7 a month later. Their equipment was mainly Avro 504Ks, F2Bs and DH 5s which, on 5 August 1918, combined to form No 33 Training Depot Station here until dis-

141

A Dakota IV KK138 *during a paradrop exercise at Weston.* (Via J. R. Norris.)

bandment in 1919.

Witney remained dormant until the 1930s when civil flying commenced. The main office block of the pre-war flying school was by the old A40 road. On the outbreak of war the airfield was taken over by Brize Norton, 2 SFTS using it as an RLG for Oxfords, one of which, *P6796*, crashed on the airfield on 2 February 1940. In the spring of 1940 de Havilland opened a Civilian Repair Unit here. The company acquired the site to relieve the main Hatfield works of repairing the multiplicity of types of de Havilland light aircraft doing war service as well as Hawker Hurricanes.

On 22 November 1940, at 05:30, an attack was made upon Witney, a raider releasing two bombs, one of which fell behind a brewery and the other in the church grounds. Some 200 houses were damaged, army vehicles on the church green were burnt and many shop windows in the high street fragmented. The damage was out of proportion to the bomb load. Witney works, though, was unscathed. Making maximum use of the site, a Royal Army Ordnance Corps Depot was built in 1941 on its western side.

By then work particularly centred upon the de Havilland Dominie and impressed Rapides. Some production work connected with the former was undertaken here. In September 1942, Brush Electrical secured a contract to build Dominies, the DH Witney staff playing a major part in initiating production. Witney works at this time was completing much of the final DH contract for 150 Dominies.

During 1943 some Brush-built aircraft were transferred to Witney for completion and at the end of the war a number of Dominies, built at Loughborough, were brought to Witney for conversion to civilian Rapide specifications. Witney also converted military Dominies to civil standards, and gave in-service backing.

During the Second World War a wide assortment of de Havilland aeroplanes came to Witney for overhaul including Tiger Moths. Some Dominoes were completed here.

The factory closed in 1946. In 1951 Smiths Industries established a factory on the one-time airfield. A surviving First World War hangar complete with Belfast Truss Roofing, was then demolished. Some First World relics remain — among them the MT depot, and airmen's hospital and the stop butts.

DID YOU KNOW ...?

— Flying from Oxfordshire commenced over 200 years ago. On 4 October 1784 the first English aeronaut, James Sadler, made the first flight from the county in a 170 ft circumference Montgolfier-type hot air balloon, only a year after the first balloon flight (from Paris on 15 October 1783). He was making one of the first balloon flights in Britain, an Italian, Vincenzo Lunardi, having made the first flight in Britain on 15 September 1784 by ascending from Moorfields in London and landing near Ware, Hertfordshire.

— Much early flying took place in southern England, the first flight being made on 5 October 1908 by S. F. Cody who flew from Laffan's Plain, Farnborough. Whether they had permission or not, several of the first British aviators made use of Oxford's Port Meadow. On 19 May 1911 Hubert Latham, a Balliol graduate, landed his Antoinette Monoplane there after a flight from Brooklands.

— The military aviation potential of Port Meadow was quickly appreciated by the Army, but the first military man intent upon sampling the field on 14 June 1911 encountered such strong winds that he was forced instead to land his 50 hp Gnôme Farman on Bessels Leigh polo ground. Next day he left for Salisbury but strong winds forced him down at Heathercroft, near Wallingford, where the aircraft was badly damaged during a rough landing.

— Activity from Port Meadow in 1911 suffered a harsh shock when in November — at which time the Imperial Aero Club was about to take over the site — an aircraft shed was battered by a fierce gale along with the fifteen aeroplanes inside. Damage was estimated at £8,000, a considerable sum in those days.

— The modern desire to achieve man-powered flight continues that of former days. In November 1911 Mr Perey Fawdrey apparently achieved his first ornithorpter lift-off. Taking off downhill near Oxford in his 10 ft 7 in span, 30 lb aircraft, he is reputed to have successfully made ten flights.

— Power Meadow was used by military aircraft in 1912, including naval machines.

— Easter Monday 1912 saw one of many balloons ascents in the area when Frank Widdenham Gooden, of Betts Aircraft, demonstrated his balloon, 'Enchantress', to 1,000 onlookers. Before the year was out Oxfordshire's folk had been treated to a German, Gustav Humel, demonstrating aerobatics at Banbury and Chipping Norton.

— The first British military aviator to be killed while flying was Second Lieutenant E. Hotchkiss, Chief Flying Instructor at Brooklands for the Bristol Aeroplane Company. On 9 September 1912 he was flying a

Bristol Monoplane when it suffered structural failure and crashed near
Oxford.

— By autumn 1912 Mr Gooden was also flying his 'Dragonfly', a 650
lb aeroplane powered by a 35-50 hp eight-cylinder JAP engine which
enabled it to fly at over 60 mph. To a newspaper reporter Gooden
confided (doubtless for publication) that he dreamed 'of travelling at
the enormous rate of 360 mph'.

— It was Easter Monday, 1913, when Oxfordians had a splendid view
of the Army airship *Beta*. Carrying five people, the first dirigible to
appear over Oxford circled Port Meadow before heading off to the
east. Wednesday 28 May 1913 brought good views of another airship,
Gamma, as it followed the course of the Thames before landing in
Blenheim Park.

— At midday on 5 August 1913 fire gutted five aircraft sheds on Port
Meadow. That effectively halted private flying there and paved the
way for the military to move in.

— In September 1913 during Army manoeuvres No 3 Squadron, RFC,
used the site and also a meadow at Weston-on-the-Green which
opened its long, illogical career as an airfield. Airships landed in
Blenheim Park a number of times. On the Friday of the exercises
residents of Oxford had a dangerously close view of the dirigible *Delta*
in difficulties. After leaving Farnborough for Rugby, trouble with a
propeller was encountered and the crew thought that a crash on High
Street, Oxford to be inevitable. Instead, *Delta* forced landed in the east
of the city among croquet and tennis players who snatched its guide
ropes to allow the crew to safely disembark. Following repairs it
departed for Rugby the following day.

— Civilian performers also visited Oxford, among them Mr Hucks,
famous for his invention of an engine starter. Between 26 and 28
February 1914 he performed aerobatic displays from a meadow by
Whitehouse Road, Grand Pont. At the time of his arrival he had
completed 170 loops, and added another 27 during the three day stint
at Oxford, eleven in the course of one flight. He also offered passenger
flights in two Bleriots, in one of which he had won the aerial Derby
around London.

— Port Meadow was used in the First World War as both a general
military training area and an airfield. In December 1917 No 34 Training
Squadron arrived from Castle Bromwich and, in August 1918, was
renamed 44 Training Squadron. On 1 April 1918 No 71 Training
Squadron had arrived and this was amalgamated with the new 44
Training Squadron. Training Squadrons also functioned at Witney.

— Building of Bicester and Upper Heyford commenced in 1917, then
both closed in 1920 only to reopen, on retained War Department
ground, in the mid-1920s. Bomber stations, they were protected by

the 1924 Fighting Area belt extending from Peterborough to Weston-Super-Mare via London. By 1926, relations with France improving, British re-armament was slowed and the third bomber station in the region, Abingdon, did not open until 1 September 1932. The new Upper Heyford had opened on 12 October 1927 and Bicester in January 1928.

— Among the types of aircraft to initially enter RAF service in Oxfordshire was the Fairey Gordon, a general-purpose light bomber based on the successful Fairey III series. Another was the Handley Page Heyford, a strange looking aeroplane due to its fuselage being attached beneath its upper mainplane, and its wheels placed in gigantic spats. Belying its antique appearance the Heyford performed quite well, and was still in service (but not in the county) during the Munich crisis. Indeed, some were scheduled to bomb Berlin. Safe return would have been almost impossible.

— Far more rare was the RAF's only Boulton & Paul Overstrand squadron, No 101, which operated from Bicester.

— On 1 May 1936 No 1 (Bomber) Group was formed, and soon took control of Abingdon, Bicester and Upper Heyford. Now the most common aircraft type to be seen was the Hawker Hind.

— Building of the expansion period aerodromes was underway in 1936. Large tracts of land needed to be levelled, huge underground fuel tanks built, tall water towers erected enabling sufficient water pressure to be ensured for supply to camps the sizes of villages. Air Ministry was well aware of ill-informed public opposition to all things military, and so every possible effort was made to ensure that the new aerodromes caused minimum disturbance, had stylish buildings and toned in with their surroundings as much as possible. The height of the 150 ft wide 300 ft long 'C' Type bomber aircraft sheds was therefore kept to a minimum, their functional design including giant windows allowing any internal bomb blast to readily escape. Gabled roofing was chosen to encourage bombs to skip along and on to the ground, then explode harmlessly. Other buildings were designed to have Georgian appearance, and the results were pleasing as witness the splendid one-time Officers' Mess at Bicester, now Cherwell College. To disguise the water tank sitting high upon steel stilts, the entire structure was encased in a brick tower. Chimneys, too, had brickwork around to improve their appearance. Such buildings were constructed with the strength to withstand assault and could well stand for a very long time. Future generations will surely judge them vastly superior and greatly more attractive than the hideous structures erected since the mid-20th Century.

— In addition to satellite airfields, training stations usually had RLGs (Relief Landing Grounds) which relieved pressure from main stations allowing a faster rate of training. Night flying from RLGs and other grass airfields involved the use of floodlights and white Glim lights, with gooseneck and money flares serving in misty weather. A main Chance floodlight illuminated the runway, red Glim lights marked obstructions, an illuminated 'T' indicated wind direction and yellow Glim lights marked the extremities of the safe landing run. Taxying post lights indicated the direction of the flare path. Such complicated lighting was not easy to extinguish when intruders were about, hence its use mainly at unsophisticated satellite airfields and RLGs in preference to main elaborate airfields.

— Vast RAF expansion between April 1939 and March 1940 was obvious around Oxford. At the start of that period about 450 aircraft were based in the county. A year later some 1,250 were there and five Operational Training Units (OTUs) had been formed.

— Orders were given on 8 August 1940 for OTUs to commence Operation Nickel, the dropping of propaganda leaflets at night on Occupied France.

— Partly pre-fabricated buildings were erected on wartime airfields to speed their construction. After the pre-war expansion aerodromes were completed construction of simpler airfields began, these often having flat roofed buildings lacking the grace of the pre-war stations. They were also characterized by Type J hangars partly made of metal and with curved roofing. Most airfields completed after 1941 had Tees Bridge's Type T (ie Transportable) or Bellman steel hangars, whose length was governed by the number of bays erected. The most common construction consisted of 23 bays making an overall length of 239 ft 7 inches. Usually the T2 sheds had ends opening to a width of 113 ft and a height of 25 ft. Many personnel accommodation huts were of the Maycrete pre-fabricated type, metal Nissen huts 36 ft long and 16 ft wide or more elaborate Laing or wooden huts. Water towers also consisted of prefabricated metal sections.

— Wartime built airfields intended for bomber and transport aircraft generally had three runways. One was of 2,000 yds length 50 yds width and two of 1,200 yds × 50 yds at many bases. Firm ground 75 yards wide flanked either side of electrically illuminated hard runways. Connecting hardstandings to the runways posed considerable problems as heavy aircraft leaving dispersal areas needed often to travel considerable distances along the perimeter track to the runway prior to take off. Such travelling was very costly in terms of fuel and time taken, especially when practice take-off and landing was involved, caused congestion and reduced levels of training efficiency not to mention the additional effect of inclement weather. Precise alignment of runways needed to take into account safest approach lines, chosen on the basis that no obstruction must rise above a path slope of 1:15 to the runway threshold. Little wonder that each aerodrome had unique qualities. Although similar, aerodrome layouts were never identical.

— At airfields with only grass surfaces policy called for three or four mown strips each 40 yd wide to serve as runways. Grass had some advantages over metalled runways, except in winter when muddy surfaces brought problems. Light aircraft did not need tarmac/concrete runways and most training stations never had them although some acquired varying amounts of Sommerfeld Mat steel tracking or Pierced Steel Planking.

— Airfields were organized into flying ground, technical site, operational areas, weapons and domestic sites. The latter were widely dispersed at wartime airfields. At pre-war stations the various functions were in clearly defined areas with aircraft being taken into hangars after the days flying. On wartime airfields aircraft were dispersed around the perimeter, initially hard ground and sometimes among trees, then on circular or tarmac pans. Mid-war saw the construction of what were known as Loop Hardstandings, to either side of the perimeter track.

— Most airfields had a selection of metal frame and panelled 'Blister' hangars. A variety of types existed, the most common being the 60 ft wide base Miskins Standard Blister, eleven of which were placed at Shellingford. At Weston-on-the Green were situated 69 ft base Blister hangars, some of which were placed end on end to produce the Double Blister. Largest of all were the Extra Over Blister type and the Dorman Long type with a 90 ft wide base. Canvas cover frames were part of the Bessoneau hangars, based on the World War 1 design and still in use up to the 1970s.

— Aircraft Storage Units had quite individualistic buildings. Large, angular looking hangars with curved roofs, known as Type D, were the norm. Examples of these can still be seen at Brize Norton and also some grass-roofed mound-like hangars, Lamella type, in which aircraft were housed against air attack. At SLGs (Satellite Landing Grounds), small, much-camouflaged sites for the storage of aircraft to reduce the number in ASUs, small hangars of the Robin type, disguised to look like farm buildings, were found as at No 22 SLG Barnsley Park, No 28 SLG Barton Abbey and No 34 SLG Woburn all for a time controlled by 6 MU Brize Norton.

— Training schemes were repeatedly adjusted during the war to take account of operational requirements and losses. At the start of 1940 a pilot left EFTS after eight weeks flying to undergo sixteen weeks at an advanced flying school. His operational training lasted six weeks if he was selected for bombers, four if he was training for fighters. Summer 1940 saw drastic reductions in flying training hours — soon after those of January had been deemed far too short!

— Average strength of an Oxfordshire bomber OTU early 1941 was about fifty bomber aircraft supplemented by Ansons for navigation training and a few gunnery aircraft. A sizeable portion of the entire bomber production was thus needed just to equip non-operational units occupying many airfields. To make OTUs productive an 'Advanced Training Area' encompassing part of northern France was designated in February 1941 over which operational flying training would take place. Satellite airfields would now be planned to operate a bomber squadron and house up to 600 men. Making the OTUs of even more operational value, on 9 July 1942 Bomber Command authorized them to carry at their discretion two 250 or 500 lb HE bombs on each *Nickel* sortie.

— A very important task variously undertaken from Harwell, Hampstead Norris and Bicester during the war was the overseas delivery of Wellingtons, Bostons and Blenheim Vs eventually by special Ferry Training Flights. Chosen crews would accustom themselves to the particular aeroplane allocated before setting off in it on the night journey to Gibraltar, or across France to Malta and Egypt. Take off was often hazardous because the aircraft would be very heavily laden with more fuel than usual. Enemy fighters had to be faced, a task the like of which few had previous experience of.

— By the end of 1941 much basic and advanced flying training was being undertaken overseas and within the Empire Air Training Scheme. Early in 1942 all Service Flying Training Schools except two in Britain switched to providing acclimatization training for aircrew who had yet to experience the variable weather conditions in northwest Europe. After twelve weeks basic service training a pilot at this time flew 60 hours during elementary flying at an EFTS such as Shellingford before being sent to an overseas hostile-free environment for a further 120 hours of more advanced flying training. After returning to Britain a bomber pilot flew 60 hours at an Advanced Flying Unit (Pilot), or 30 hours if he was a fighter trainee.

— Since OTUs like those at Harwell, Upper Heyford and Abingdon held only twin-engined aircraft, bomber pilots needed a further 30 hours conversion training onto four-engined bombers at Heavy Conversion Units. Demands on OTUs by early 1942 were enormous for the plan was to establish within the RAF 156 'heavy' bomber squadrons and 86 'medium' bomber squadrons for which the Oxfordshire OTUs would need to provide a goodly proportion and a continuous supply of crews. To train the vast number of men needed was an enormous, skilled and very costly task. It was slightly reduced when on 29 March 1942 a change was introduced to the effect that in future each heavy bomber would have only one pilot as with the

Lancaster. At Upper Heyford, 16 OTU already functioned along those lines since the Hampden needed only one pilot. When that type was phased out it was replaced at the OTU by the Wellington.

— Few bombing missions were flown from Oxfordshire but for the 'Thousand Plane' raid on Cologne on 30 May 1942 its OTUs despatched 83 aircraft. The raid enormously raised morale in the OTUs and gave crews a brief taste of the troubles in store for them. But many of their aircraft were not fully up-to-date, few pupils had sufficient training as a team, and the weapons used were inadequate and dated. Each OTU had flown about 500 hours in training and preparation for the raid — a highly costly feature. For the 1,000 bomber Essen raid of 1 June the Oxfordshire OTUs despatched 84 aircraft of which two did not return. Against Bremen on 25 June they despatched another 72 bombers and lost six. At dawn on 26 June Blenheims of 13 OTU carried out a search for aircrew adrift in dinghies in the North Sea, the only time between 1939 and 1945 when aircraft from Bicester could ever be said to have carried out operational sorties.

— Friday 30 August 1940 witnessed some of the toughest fighting of the Battle of Britain. In the third, large-scale afternoon phase of the day enemy formations set out to demolish factories at Oxford and Luton. Luckily the He 111s heading for Oxford were intercepted over Surrey and turned back.

Oxfordshire played a far more prominent part in the Battle of Britain than might at first seem to be the case. Not only were many Spitfires brought to the Morris Cowley works for rapid repair, others also were taken to the deHavilland Witney works for similar treatment. To Witney also went many Hurricanes damaged in battle or in accidents, such repairs being undertaken almost to the end of the war. A major part in repairing Battle of Britain Hurricanes was also undertaken by Air Training, the company working intensively throughout the summer fighting to return Hurricanes to the RAF. Once the fierce fight was over some Hurricanes were stored, engineless, at selected sites reckoned safe from enemy attention. No 15 MU and Air Training were to re-engine these aircraft and return them to flying state. Some were later used by the Fleet Air Arm and a few even found their way to the USSR.

— Four V-1 flying bombs fell on Oxfordshire, the first two coming down on 21 June 1944 at Nuffield near Benson and at Maiden. One fell at Checkendon on 5 July and the last at Stonor on 20 August.

— A great moment of glory came to Stanton Harcourt in January 1943 when Mr Winston Churchill set off in his famous Liberator transport, AL504 'Commando' of 511 Squadron, Lyneham, for the Casablanca Conference at which he and President Roosevelt planned the massive Allied strategic bomber onslaught on Germany.

— In April 1943 what was virtually the final training scheme for bomber OTUs became effective. Hitherto the Unit was divided into four Flights in which trainees passed through each specialized section of the Unit. Under the revised system the OTU was divided into a Basic section and an Applied section, each having two bomber Flights. The Basic element was based at the satellite station, where in addition, a Flight of target towing Martinets and a handful of fighters was provided for gunnery training. Cross country flying, operational exercises and a Nickel operation were flown from the main base where the course had started with two weeks ground school training. One Nickel operation per week for up to four sorties was prescribed, each Wellington carrying twenty packets of leaflets and two bombs if necessary.

— One of the most unusual Oxfordshire airfield features was largely underground at Harwell. In 1935 design work commenced on a giant catapult for the launching of very heavily laden bombers. Space being at a premium at the Royal Aircraft Establishment, Farnborough, this Mk III catapult was sited at Harwell. A 100 ft diameter pit deep enough to contain a house was dug close to the A34 road, over which a turntable was built. Power to give the push for take off was provided by a battery of Rolls-Royce Kestrel engines. Although the device was never tried out it appears that an operator was on hand from 1939 to 1945 and was paid regularly during his long underground stint!

— Very few aircraft with wartime service in Oxfordshire have survived. The most distinguished is the Percival Gull Six G-ADPR alias AX866 which was the aircraft in which the famous Miss Jean Batten made record flights. It joined No 4 Glider Training School at Kidlington serving that School from 8 April 1942 and subsequently being used by 20 (P) AFU until October 1943. Presently the aircraft is in the hands of the Shuttleworth Collection at Old Warden. Another survivor is the Miles Whitney Straight G-AERV which as EM999 was based at Abingdon between 24 July 1941 and 28 May 1945. It is now exhibited in the Ulster Folk and Transport Museum.

SUMMARY OF BASIC FEATURES OF WARTIME MILITARY OXFORDSHIRE AIRFIELDS IN JANUARY 1945

Hangars (Type and number)	Runways (Direction, and dimensions in yards)	Hardstandings (Type and number)
Abingdon A – 4 C – 1	027/207 1,600×50 190/010 2,000×50 (concrete)	Spectacle – 6 Frying pan – 24
Akeman Street Bellman – 1 65 ft Blister – 10	N/S 1,100 NE/SW 950 SE/NW 800 (grass)	None
Barford St John T2 – 1 B1 – 1	170/350 1,400×50 216/036 1,400×50 281/101 2,000×50 (concrete)	Heavy bomber – 27
Benson C – 4 Over Blister – 3 Extra Over Blister – 4	069/249 1,990×50 020/200 1,420×50 (concrete and wood chips)	120 ft diam – 10
Bicester A – 2 B – 2	NW/SE 1,200 SW/NE 1,100 (grass)	Tarmac – 41
Brize Norton C – 4, D – 2, E – 2 T2 – 5, Lamella – 6 Blister – 2, Over Blister – 5, Blister Robin – 15, Bellman – 2, Bellman Oversize – 1	224/046 2,000×50 266/086 3,000×50 (concrete and wood chips)	None

Hangars (Type and number)	Runways (Direction and dimensions in yards)	Hardstandings (Type and number)
Broadwell T2 – 2	190/010 2,000×50 070/250 1,400×50 310/140 1,400×50 (concrete, wood chip covering)	48 Concrete aprons – 2
Chalgrove T2 – 2	140/320 2,000×50 250/070 1,400×50 190/010 1,400×50 (tarmac and concrete)	Loop – 50
Chipping Norton Bellman – 2 65 ft Blister – 10	117/297 1,010 064/206 760 (Sommerfeld track)	None
Culham 87 ft×60 ft – 21 185 ft×105 ft – 11	06/24 1,200×30 10/28 1,400×30 17/35 1,200×30	16
Edgehill T2 – 1 B1 – 1	172/352 1,540×50 239/059 1,100×50 284/104 1,100×50 (tarmac and concrete)	Heavy bomber – 27
Enstone T2 – 1 B1 – 1	195/015 1,200×50 256/076 2,000×50 329/149 1,200×50 (concrete)	Heavy bomber – 27
Finmere T2 – 1 B1 – 1	280/100 2,000×50 230/050 1,400×50 162/342 1,400×50 (concrete and wood chips)	Frying pan – 27

Hangars (Type and number)	Runways (Direction and dimensions in yards)	Hardstandings (Type and number)
Grove T2 - 6	220/040 2,000×50 340/160 1,400×50 270/090 1,200×50 (concrete)	Frying pan - 24 Spectacle - 26
Harwell C - 4	151/331 1,300×50 258/078 1,400×50 295/115 2,000×50 (concrete)	Tarmac - 10 Concrete - 45
Kelmscot Enlarged Over Blister - 1	E/W 1,400 NW/SE 1,000 (grass)	None
Kidlington None	N/S 1,026	None
Kidlington Bellman - 7 Horace - 1 Blister - 10	024/204 1,140 (grass) 351/171 1,140 (grass) 286/106 1,312 (Army tracking)	Rectangular - 4
Kingston Bagpuize Butler - 2 T2 -1 Blister (large) - 2 Blister (small) - 1	020/200 2,400×50 080/260 1,400×50 1,400×50 (PSP)	Pierced Steel Planking - 50
Mount Farm Blister 69 ft - 4 Blister 65 ft - 4	170/350 1,100×50 120/100 1,100×50 240/060 1,600×50 (asphalt)	Loop - 24
Shellingford Bellman - 4 Blister - 11	NE/SW 1,150 E/W 1,025 NW/SE 933 (grass)	None

Hangars (Type and number)	Runways (Direction and dimensions in yards)	Hardstandings (Type and number)
Stanton Harcourt T2 – 1 B1 – 1	056/236 1,600×50 177/357 1,100×50 117/297 1,100×50 (tarmac)	Heavy bomber – 27
Upper Heyford A6	217/037 2,000×50 264/084 1,700×50 311/139 1,550×50 (concrete)	Loop – 7 Frying pan – 23
Watchfield Bellman – 5 Over Blister – 5	NW/SE 1,400 NNW/SSE 1,700 N/S 900 (grass)	Concrete roads – 11
Weston-on-the-Green T2 – 1 Bessoneau (9 bay) – 2 Bessoneau (12 bay) – 2 Double 69 ft Blister – 4 Single 69 ft Blister – 6	265/085 1,500 210/030 1,200 (Sommerfeld tracking)	None

INDEX